Civil Rights Implications of Post-September 11 Law Enforcement Practices in New York

**New York Advisory Committee to
the U.S. Commission on Civil Rights**

March 2004

The United States Commission on Civil Rights

The U.S. Commission on Civil Rights is an independent, bipartisan agency established by Congress in 1957, reconstituted in 1983, and reauthorized in 1994. It is directed to investigate complaints alleging that citizens are being deprived of their right to vote by reason of their race, color, religion, sex, age, disability, or national origin, or by reason of fraudulent practices; study and collect information relating to discrimination or a denial of equal protection of the laws under the Constitution because of race, color, religion, sex, age, disability, or national origin, or in the administration of justice; appraise federal laws and policies with respect to discrimination or denial of equal protection of the laws because of race, color, religion, sex, age, disability, or national origin, or in the administration of justice; serve as a national clearinghouse for information in respect to discrimination or denial of equal protection of the laws because of race, color, religion, sex, age, disability, or national origin; submit reports, findings, and recommendations to the President and Congress; and issue public service announcements to discourage discrimination or denial of equal protection of the laws.

The State Advisory Committees

By law, the U.S. Commission on Civil Rights has established an advisory committee in each of the 50 states and the District of Columbia. The committees are composed of state citizens who serve without compensation. The committees advise the Commission of civil rights issues in their states that are within the Commission's jurisdiction. More specifically, they are authorized to advise the Commission on matters of their state's concern in the preparation of Commission reports to the President and the Congress; receive reports, suggestions, and recommendations from individuals, public officials, and representatives of public and private organizations to committee inquiries; forward advice and recommendations to the Commission, as requested; and observe any open hearing or conference conducted by the Commission in their states.

Civil Rights Implications of Post-September 11 Law Enforcement Practices in New York

Letter of Transmittal

New York Advisory Committee to
the U.S. Commission on Civil Rights

Members of the Commission
Mary Frances Berry, *Chairperson*
Cruz Reynoso, *Vice Chairperson*
Jennifer C. Braceras
Christopher Edley, Jr.
Peter N. Kirsanow
Elsie M. Meeks
Abigail Thernstrom
Russell G. Redenbaugh

Les Jin, *Staff Director*

Shortly after the September 11 tragedies, the U.S. Commission on Civil Rights urged its State Advisory Committees to monitor possible civil rights violations in their states against Muslims, Sikhs, Arabs, and South Asians. The New York Advisory Committee submits this report, *Civil Rights Implications of Post-September 11 Law Enforcement Practices in New York*, as part of its responsibility to advise the Commission on civil rights issues within the state. The report was adopted by the Advisory Committee by a 14 to 0 vote, with three members abstaining.

In December 2002, the Committee identified as its most pressing concern the question of whether civil rights were being violated in New York by federal and local security measures implemented after the terrorist attacks. The Committee decided to hold a community forum in New York City on May 21, 2003. Presentations were made to the Committee from 18 persons in three panels, which explored such issues as racial profiling by law enforcement, special federal registration requirements for foreign nationals from predominantly Islamic countries, and the civil rights implications of expanded government powers under the USA Patriot Act.

This report summarizes the panelists' statements and expresses concerns and observations based on the information received. The Advisory Committee trusts the Commission and the public will find the material in this report informative.

Sincerely,

Michael Hanley, *Chairperson*
New York Advisory Committee

New York Advisory Committee to the U.S. Commission on Civil Rights

Michael Hanley, *Chairperson*
Rochester

Leslie B. Anderson
Central Islip

Emilio Fuentes
Buffalo

Stephen E. Gottlieb
Albany

Kimberly Hardy
New York

Joan B. Johnson
Islip

Ghazi Y. Khankan
Westbury

Gloria Lopez
Rochester

Paul D. Q. Nguyen
New York

Setsuko Matsunaga Nishi
Tappan

Elizabeth R. OuYang
Brooklyn

Gregory Rabb
Jamestown

Lita Taracido
New York

Norman Wagner
Central Islip

Thomas R. Wahl, Jr.
Rochester

Cecile C. Weich
Bronx

David Alan Wright
Buffalo

Acknowledgments

The New York Advisory Committee wishes to thank the staff of the Commission's Eastern Regional Office—Ivy Davis, acting regional director, Ki-Taek Chun, now retired regional director, and Aonghas St-Hilaire—for their assistance in planning and executing the forum and in preparing and producing the report. Dawn Sweet provided editorial services. Dorothy Pearson-Canty and Alfreda Greene provided production and distribution services.

The Committee gratefully acknowledges the assistance given in convening the May 21, 2003, community forum by the New York University (NYU) School of Law, and in particular the NYU Asian/Pacific/American Studies Program and Institute and the NYU Institute for Law and Society.

Contents

[blank page]

Executive Summary

The New York Advisory Committee's May 2003 community forum on post-September 11 civil rights issues was organized in three panels. In Panel 1, the Committee examined the civil rights implications and social consequences of racial profiling in law enforcement before and after 9/11. In Panels 2 and 3, the Committee explored the closely related questions of whether security measures adopted in connection with federal registration of nonimmigrants (defined as anyone not yet a citizen or permanent resident of the United States and applies to visitors, students, temporary workers, and temporary residents), border crossings of nonimmigrants from New York into Canada, and the surveillance of religious and political organizations—measures targeted at particular racial and ethnic populations—have violated the civil rights of members of Muslim, Arab, and South Asian communities in New York. Moreover, the Committee considered whether these heightened security measures may have actually been counterproductive to the interests of increasing national security.

Panel participants presented testimony as representatives of advocacy groups who work regularly with persons affected by the policy changes or in the protection of civil rights, or as individuals directly affected by post-9/11 law enforcement policies and practices. In addition, panelists appeared on behalf of the following government agencies: the New York State Attorney General's Office, the Bureau of Customs and Border Protection of the U.S. Department of Homeland Security, and the state Committee on Open Government (an office of the New York Department of State). The New York City Police Department, the Transportation Security Administration offices for the LaGuardia and JFK airports, and the New York City office of the Bureau of Citizenship and Immigration Services of the U.S. Department of Homeland Security were invited to appear, but were unable to attend the forum.

Set forth below are summaries of key points made by the forum presenters. More detail related to these concerns follows throughout the report.

1. In the aftermath of 9/11, it was important that law enforcement authorities at all levels of government take steps to respond to the threat of terrorism. However, some actions have adversely affected the civil rights of immigrants and nonimmigrants, particularly members of Muslim, Arab, and South Asian communities. Policies of particular concern are the federal government's expanded authority to detain nonimmigrants without charge, to hold detainees with no possibility for release on bond, and, when final deportation orders have been issued, to subject detainees to prolonged confinement. Other policies of concern are the federal government's Call-In Special Registration program and sharing of national databases on immigration status with state and local police.

2. There are parallels between the racial profiling of Japanese Americans during World War II, pre-9/11 profiling of African Americans and Hispanic Americans, and post-9/11 profiling of Muslims, Arabs, and South Asians. Racial profiling has been statistically proven by government studies, including the New York State Attorney General's 1999 study of

stop-and-frisk practices, to be an ineffective law enforcement tool for identifying criminal conduct. Much racial profiling of African Americans and Latinos continues unnoticed in the post-9/11 law enforcement environment. Beyond law enforcement acts of racial profiling related to drug prevention and street crime, racial profiling has taken on new dimensions targeting Muslims, Arabs, and South Asians regarding business license violations, financial transactions abroad, and international travel at airports.

3. There is a perception that local law enforcement authorities did not take seriously the complaints of Muslim, Arab, and South Asian residents who were subjected to hate crimes in acts of misplaced retaliation for the events of September 11. This has been an issue in the taxi industry, where many drivers are South Asian in origin. In the immediate months following 9/11, South Asian taxi drivers found themselves particularly vulnerable to attacks and in need of police protection.

4. The federal Call-In Special Registration program requiring male nationals 16 years and older from predominantly Muslim countries to register is seen by some as a form of racial profiling, targeting Muslims, Arabs, and South Asians. The program ceased after nationals from predominantly Muslim countries had registered.

5. In New York City, implementation of the Call-In Special Registration program was marked by a lack of community education on the program's requirements, excessive processing times lasting 14 hours or more, lack of sufficiently trained interviewers and translators, and inconsistent application of policies.

6. Persons required to undergo special registration in New York City were deprived of the right to counsel while interrogated by the investigations unit of the Bureau of Immigration and Customs Enforcement of the U.S. Department of Homeland Security (formerly the Immigration and Naturalization Service), when they were most vulnerable. If registrants were placed in detention, families were not informed of their whereabouts.

7. Refugee shelter advocates pointed to fear of how the Call-In Special Registration program was being implemented as the main impetus for the flight of Muslims, Arabs, and South Asians from the United States into Canada via Buffalo or Plattsburg, New York, in search of asylum. Canadian immigration authorities, overwhelmed by the number of refugees, sent many asylum seekers back to the United States. In the United States, many Canadian-bound asylum seekers were placed in deportation proceedings with excessive bonds reported as a condition of release. Their detention and deportation from the United States effectively denied them the protection of and access to the Canadian immigration system.

8. The federal government's new policy of sharing national databases on immigration status with state and local police could undermine effective law enforcement. Undocumented immigrants may fail to report crimes or suspicious behavior to law enforcement officials for fear of negative reprisals based on their immigration status. This deprives law enforcement authorities of an important community-based source of crime-fighting information.

9. The creation of joint terrorism task forces allowing for greater cooperation and the sharing of information between federal and local law enforcement authorities and the recent court dilution of the *Handschu* consent decree, which eliminates the civilian oversight component in approving local police surveillance of political organizations, are issues of concern.

In sum, the law enforcement policies and practices described above pose a threat to civil rights and civil liberties, especially within New York's Muslim, Arab, and South Asian communities. These programs may be counterproductive. They fuel distrust of law enforcement authorities among many members of affected communities, hinder local reporting of crimes, and diminish the cooperation between local police and community members necessary to identify and thwart future terrorists.

Chapter 1: Background

Racial and ethnic profiling has a long history in the United States. For example, during post-Reconstruction years in the South white vigilantes kept peremptory watch over African Americans,[1] using the Black Codes and vagrancy laws to legitimize their actions.[2] As a further example, after the Japanese attack on Pearl Harbor in 1941 federal authorities forced 120,000 men, women, and children of Japanese ancestry into internment camps, equating ethnicity with collective guilt.[3] More recently and for many years, African Americans, Latinos, and others have complained that they are subject to unwarranted police scrutiny in their cars and on the streets. Their complaints have often been ignored.[4] Throughout its long and torturous history, the practice of racial and ethnic profiling has been a thorn in police-community relations, fostering distrust and tension where trust and cooperation could feasibly prevail.

Longstanding practices of profiling notwithstanding, by the mid-1990s—but before the events of September 11—police and lawmakers were beginning to acknowledge that racial profiling exists and to condemn it as wrong.[5] The American public, too, was increasingly aware of the existence and inappropriateness of profiling. In 2000, for example, approximately 80 percent of Americans surveyed indicated that they had heard of racial profiling and expressed the opinion that it should be stopped.[6] Reflecting the growing awareness among policy makers and the public, the Civil Rights Division of the U.S. Department of Justice began to sue local police departments where it found egregious patterns and practices of racial and ethnic profiling.[7]

The terrorist attacks of September 11, 2001, shattered the emerging public consensus that racial and ethnic profiling is wrong and should be eliminated. Less than a month after the attacks, a majority of Americans surveyed supported greater scrutiny of Arabs. Indeed, most white, black, and other non-white Americans expressed support of profiling of Arabs at airports and of requiring Arabs to carry special identification cards.[8]

Although profiling of Arabs and Muslims was a concern before 9/11, its scope and impact expanded dramatically after the terrorist attacks. A poll conducted in May 2002 found that more than three-

---

[1] Tanya E. Coke, "Racial Profiling Post-9/11: Old Story, New Debate," in *Lost Liberties*, ed. Cynthia Brown (New York: The New Press, 2003), p. 91.

[2] Eric Foner, *Reconstruction: America's Unfinished Revolution* (New York: Harper & Row, 1988), pp. 199–201.

[3] Stanley Mark, Suzette Brooks Masters, and Cyrus Mehta, "Have We Learned the Lessons of History?" *Immigration Policy Focus*, vol. 1, issue 3 (January 2003).

[4] Leadership Conference on Civil Rights Education Fund, *Wrong Then, Wrong Now: Racial Profiling Before and After September 11, 2001*, February 2003.

[5] Coke, "Racial Profiling Post-9/11," p. 91.

[6] Gallup Organization, "Racial Profiling Is Seen as Widespread, Particularly Among Young Black Men," Dec. 9, 1999.

[7] Coke, "Racial Profiling Post-9/11," p. 91. *See* appendix for Department of Justice's *Fact Sheet on Racial Profiling*.

[8] Gallup Organization, "Terrorism Most Important, But Americans Remain Upbeat," Oct. 18. 2001.

quarters of Arab Americans felt that there was more profiling of Arab Americans since 9/11, and nearly two-thirds felt very or somewhat worried about the long-term effects of discrimination.[9] Reports by other State Advisory Committees to the U.S. Commission on Civil Rights confirm the existence of post-9/11 racial and ethnic profiling, as well as a surge in hate violence and discrimination in the United States against people who are or are perceived to be Arab, South Asian, or Muslim in the months immediately following 9/11.[10]

Commentators and others have linked increased post-9/11 profiling of Arabs, South Asians, and Muslims in part to changes in federal policy since the attacks.[11] The USA Patriot Act, for example, was signed into existence one month after the terrorist attacks.[12] It is designed to give new powers to the federal government to fight terrorism. It gives federal agents greater authority to track and intercept communications and financial transactions, expanding the power of the Secretary of the Treasury to regulate the activities of U.S. financial institutions, especially their relations with foreign nationals and entities. The act also contains a number of provisions affecting immigration policy, particularly regarding the comings and goings of nonimmigrants—for example, students, temporary workers, and temporary residents. These provisions enable authorities to detain and deport nonimmigrants suspected of being terrorists.[13]

The National Security Entry/Exit Registration System (NSEERS) was implemented on September 11, 2002, to better track the whereabouts of nonimmigrants.[14] For male nonimmigrants 16 years of age and older already in the United States, federal authorities established the Call-In Special Registration program. Call-In Special Registration required that male nonimmigrants from a list of targeted countries report to the Bureau of Citizenship and Immigration Services (BCIS) of the U.S. Department of Homeland Security (DHS) [formerly the Immigration and Naturalization Service (INS)] to be fingerprinted and photographed, and to answer detailed questions under oath.[15]

BCIS designated Call-In Groups of nonimmigrants to register. Group 1 included nationals from Iran, Iraq, Libya, Sudan, and Syria; Group 2 included nationals from Afghanistan, Algeria, Bahrain, Eritrea, Lebanon, Morocco, North Korea, Oman, Qatar, Somalia, Tunisia, United Arab Emirates, and Yemen; Group 3 included nationals from Pakistan and Saudi Arabia; and Group 4 included nationals from Bangladesh, Egypt, Indonesia, Jordan, and Kuwait. Special registration was completed with Group 4. Only foreign nationals of predominantly Islamic countries—with the exception of North

---

[9] Arab American Institute, "Healing the Nation: The Arab American Experience After September 11" (a first anniversary report), p. 20.

[10] District of Columbia, Maryland, and Virginia Advisory Committees to the U.S. Commission on Civil Rights, *Civil Rights Concerns in the Metropolitan Washington, D.C., Area in the Aftermath of the September 11, 2001, Tragedies*, June 2003, p. 1; Illinois Advisory Committee to the U.S. Commission on Civil Rights, *Arab and Muslim Civil Rights Issues in the Chicago Metropolitan Area Post-September 11*, May 2003, p. 4.

[11] Coke, "Racial Profiling Post-9/11," p. 101; Lawyers Committee for Human Rights, *A Year of Loss: Reexamining Civil Liberties Since September 11*, 2002, pp. 13–24; Kate Martin, "Secret Arrests and Preventive Detention," in *Lost Liberties*, ed. Cynthia Brown (New York: The New Press, 2003), p. 77; Leadership Conference on Civil Rights Education Fund, *Wrong Then, Wrong Now*.

[12] Uniting and Strengthening America by Providing Appropriate Tools Required to Intercept and Obstruct Terrorism Act of 2001 (USA Patriot Act), 107 Pub. L. No. 56, 115 Stat. 272 (2001) (codified in scattered titles and sections of the U.S.C.).

[13] Charles Doyle, "The USA Patriot Act: A Sketch" (Washington, D.C.: Congressional Research Service, Apr. 18, 2002).

[14] Registration and Monitoring of Certain Nonimmigrants, 67 Fed. Reg. 40,581 (2002) (amends 8 C.F.R. parts 214 and 264).

[15] *Id*. Pearl Law Group, "Immigration Information: Special Registration," n.d., <http://www.immigrationlaw.com/ImmigrationInfo/SpecialRegistration.html>.

Korea—were required to register in the Call-In Special Registration program.[16] Because it targets primarily Muslims, many feel special registration is discriminatory, an act of racial or religious profiling.[17]

Special registration is designed to weed out potential terrorists. However, many foreign-born Muslims in New York and throughout the United States feared that they would be jailed when they showed up for processing.[18] This fear was fueled in part by the December 2002 detentions of more than 400 mostly Iranian men who appeared for special registration in Los Angeles. Most of the detainees were put into custody for deportation hearings because their visas were no longer current.[19] Many of those funneled into deportation hearings had already applied with INS to live in the United States as legal, permanent residents.[20]

New York has more than 400,000 undocumented immigrants. These people are most adversely affected by special registration requirements. If they register, they may be detained for violating immigration law. If they do not register, they are breaking the law and become deportable. They find themselves in a Catch-22 situation.[21] Of the 82,000 men nationwide who underwent special registration, about 13,400—or approximately 16 percent—face deportation.[22] Only a few of these men are suspected to have links with terrorism.[23] Critics say that those most likely to comply with special registration are honest individuals. Those with terrorist goals are the least likely to register with the program, or to truthfully answer the program's required questions.[24]

Fear of special registration led many Muslim men and their families—including those with U.S.-born children—to make the decision to leave the United States of their own accord rather than risk being detained and, especially, deported.[25] Many believed they would suffer hardship if sent back to their home countries.[26] On some blocks of certain New York City neighborhoods many shops are boarded up and abandoned by families not willing to risk perceived negative repercussions of special registration.[27] Many who decided to leave headed for Canada. The border crossings near Buffalo and particularly Plattsburgh, New York, were high-volume ports of entry into Canada for Muslim asylum seekers from the United States.

---

[16] U.S. Department of Homeland Security, Bureau of Citizenship and Immigration Services, "Special Registration," n.d., <http://www.immigration.gov/graphics/shared/lawenfor/specialreg/>. The first Call-In registrations started on November 15, 2002. The final registration period ended on March 28, 2003.

[17] Steve Orr, "Plan Creates a Muslim Exodus to Canada," *Rochester Democrat and Chronicle*, Mar. 20, 2003, p. 10A; Mark Bixler, "Caught up in Terror: INS Expels Rising Number of Illegals to Muslim Lands," *Atlanta Journal-Constitution*, Jan. 15, 2003, p. 1F.

[18] Ahmar Mustikhan and Jeff Elliott, "Pakistani Families Flee U.S. to Seek Canada Asylum," *Monitor*, Feb. 12, 2003, <http://www.monitor.net/monitor/0302a/specialregistration.html>.

[19] Patrick J. McDonnell, "Nearly 24,000 Men Register in the U.S.," *Los Angeles Times*, Jan. 19, 2003, p. 22.

[20] Emily Bazar, "New Battle on Civil Rights Front: The Registration of Some Immigrants Is Denounced as Racial Profiling," *Sacramento Bee*, Jan. 20, 2003, p. A1.

[21] Chaleampon Ritthichai, "Special Registration," *Gotham Gazette*, Mar. 3, 2002, <http://www.gothamgazette.com/article/20030324/200/324>.

[22] Tom McCann, "Special Registration Shows Key Changes," *Chicago Lawyer*, August 2003, p. 23.

[23] Haider Rizvi, "U.S.-Rights: Deportation Trap Threatens Muslim, Arab Families," *Inter Press Service*, Aug. 22, 2003.

[24] Karen Weinstock, "Honest People Pay for Anti-Terrorism Initiatives," *Atlanta-Journal Constitution*, Aug. 4, 2003, p. 13A.

[25] Mustikhan and Elliott, "Pakistani Families Flee U.S."

[26] Orr, "Plan Creates a Muslim Exodus to Canada."

[27] Ritthichai, "Special Registration."

The Pakistani community was particularly hard hit. Canadian immigration authorities reported that 2,000 Pakistanis entered Canada between January and March 2003—a figure comparable to the entire year of 2002. Moreover, many more asylum seekers were waiting at the border when the three-month 2003 statistics were compiled.[28] Because of the sheer numbers of asylum seekers, Citizenship and Immigration Canada (CIC) officials had many make appointments to come back later. Those told to make an appointment were forced back to the United States, where federal authorities were making arrests based on immigration violations.[29] Those not arrested made temporary home in refugee assistance organizations or, because of the overcrowded conditions of these organizations, had to wait elsewhere for their CIC appointment.[30]

Other federal policy changes have affected the civil rights and civil liberties of New Yorkers. One such policy change—namely, increased cooperation between federal law enforcement authorities and state and local law enforcement authorities—has repercussions for police-community relations in the state. In August 2003, for example, the federal government allowed local police to enforce immigration law for the first time. Immigrant community spokespersons have confirmed that the New York City Police Department (NYPD) has increasingly acted as an agent of federal immigration authorities.[31] Some maintain that as local police start enforcing federal immigration law, which has been traditionally treated as civil rather than criminal law, local immigrant communities will stop working with the police,[32] thereby undermining cooperative police-community relations.

Federal authorities have created special task forces of federal, state, and local law enforcement agents across the United States to help prevent future terrorist attacks.[33] In New York City, local police have

---

[28] "Muslims Flee to Canada to Escape INS Registration," *Daily Star*, Apr. 20, 2003, <http://www.thedailystar.net/daily starnews/200304/20/n3042013.htm>.

[29] Mustikhan and Elliott, "Pakistani Families Flee U.S."

In a letter dated January 20, 2004, Jason P. Ahern, assistant commissioner, Office of Field Operations, U.S. Customs and Border Protection, Department of Homeland Security, wrote that these statements address "actions taken by border agencies, both Canadian and U.S., in response to the surge in asylum applicants traveling to Canada, many of whom were out of legal immigration status in the United States. Federal authorities have a responsibility to enforce the laws of the United States and to take appropriate action when they encounter violators, and Federal agencies must often adjust their enforcement procedures and tactics in response to emergencies and trends as they occur. The Immigration and Naturalization Service (INS) and later CBP worked closely with Citizenship and Immigration Canada (CIC) and with the advocacy organizations to manage this influx as efficiently as possible in accordance with existing laws, regulations and policies."

[30] Brian Mann, "Registration Rules Prompt Some American Muslims to Seek Canadian Residence," *Voice of America News*, Apr. 14, 2003.

[31] Ritthichai, "Special Registration." In a letter dated February 3, 2004, Stephen L. Hammerman, deputy commissioner of legal matters, New York City Police Department, wrote in response to this statement: "It is untrue that the NYPD 'has increasingly acted as an agent of federal immigration.' It is untrue that the NYPD acts as an agent of federal immigration authorities. Indeed, the NYPD has not sought delegation of immigration enforcement authority from the Attorney General pursuant to 8 U.S.C. 1357 as some law enforcement agencies have. Moreover, recent Mayoral Executive Orders reiterate longstanding NYPD policy not to inquire about the immigration status of crime victims, witnesses, or others who approach the police seeking assistance. As a responsible law enforcement authority, the Department cooperates with federal agencies on joint investigations and if an individual comes into police custody who we learn is wanted for an immigration violation we will turn that person over to federal authorities. Despite the Department's request for detailed information regarding their claims, immigration advocates have provided only anecdotes on what appear to be a relatively few number of instances in which someone the Department encountered was wanted solely for an immigration violation and not an independent violation of state law."

[32] Nik Bonopartis, "Patriot Act Helps Police in Fighting Crime," *Poughkeepsie Journal*, Sept. 29, 2003, p. 1A.

[33] Richard B. Schmitt and Greg Krikorian, "Foot Soldiers on the Homeland Security Front," *Los Angeles Times*, Apr. 21, 2003, p. 18.

nearly 1,000 officers assigned to fight terrorism.[34] Under the federal-local Joint Terrorism Task Force in New York,[35] many of these officers are federally deputized and enjoy special security clearances.[36]

However, not all municipal police departments comply with federal initiatives. In Detroit, for example, the city has directed police to refrain from collecting information about one's political, religious, or social views unless such information directly relates to a criminal investigation. In addition, Montgomery County, Maryland—a northern suburb of Washington, D.C.—passed a resolution against racial and religious profiling and information gathering by local police at the urging of local citizen groups.[37]

Some civil liberties advocates are concerned about the involvement of local and state law enforcement authorities in domains traditionally the reserve of the federal government, especially intelligence work. Many question what will be done with the information gathered on those who have no links to terrorism. Some fear a return to abuses of the past when local police departments investigated and kept files on people and organizations without any evidence of a crime. Some law enforcement officials, however, express confidence that local police have learned from past mistakes and only keep intelligence information that is relevant to the fight against terrorism.[38]

Despite its persistence and heightened prevalence after 9/11, racial profiling remains far from universally accepted as a valid law enforcement technique. Like the internment of Japanese-origin persons living in the United States during World War II, the post-9/11 practice of profiling and differentially treating Muslim, Arab, and South Asian men living in the United States is a form of prejudice and an outward manifestation and consequence of stereotyping.[39]

Moreover, profiling is an ineffective law enforcement tool.[40] Soon after the 9/11 attacks, a group of senior American intelligence specialists combating terrorism argued against U.S. law enforcement agents relying on racial, ethnic, or religious profiling. Profiling adds nothing to national security and may in fact compromise it. Law enforcement authorities would better serve the American people by focusing on individual behaviors rather than ascriptive characteristics to prevent future terrorist attacks.[41]

---

[34] Rocco Parascandola, "It's Detective Work 101: 'A Team' Follows Lead from Check Kiting to Terrorism," *Newsday*, Apr. 20, 2003, p. A01.

[35] The Joint Terrorism Task Force in New York is not a new development and is not the result of stepped-up enforcement of immigration laws. It was created more than 20 years ago. However, the size of the task force grew after 9/11 to address increased concerns of terrorist threats.

[36] Phillip O'Connor, "States Are Striving to Get into Intelligence Business," *St. Louis Post-Dispatch*, Aug. 10, 2003, p. B1.

[37] Beth Gorham, "Dozens of U.S. Cities Defying Patriot Act," *Gazette*, Oct. 15, 2003, p. A29.

[38] O'Connor, "States Are Striving to Get into Intelligence Business."

[39] Mark, Masters, and Mehta, "Have We Learned the Lessons of History?"

[40] Leadership Council on Civil Rights, *Wrong Then, Wrong Now*, p. 29.

[41] Bill Dedman, "Fighting Terror/Words of Caution: Airport Security Memo Warns Against Use of Profiling as Defense," *Boston Globe*, Oct. 12, 2001, p. A27.

Chapter 2: Panel Summaries

Panel 1: Racial and Ethnic Profiling in Law Enforcement

Even though the term itself may be relatively recent, racial and ethnic profiling by law enforcement has a long history in American race relations. Unlike many other aspects of institutionalized discrimination, however, the presence of racial and ethnic profiling can be objectively determined, and it is widely accepted as wrong. Still, the issue of racial and ethnic profiling by law enforcement agencies in the context of antiterrorism activities poses hard questions. The purpose of this panel was to evaluate the ostensibly countervailing considerations of the need to ensure adequate national security and the need to protect the civil rights of individuals—particularly those of immigrants and minorities.

Panel participants addressed (1) the civil rights implications of racial profiling; (2) the extent to which increases in national security needs since 9/11 justify curtailing civil liberties, if at all; and (3) the extent to which, and with what consequences, New York's Muslim, Arab, and South Asian individuals, families, and communities have experienced racial and ethnic profiling by local and federal law enforcement authorities. Summaries of the panelists' presentations follow.[1]

King Downing, *National Coordinator, Campaign Against Racial Profiling, American Civil Liberties Union*

Mr. Downing defined racial profiling as the use of race to support a discretionary judgment by a law enforcement officer to stop, frisk, detain, search, arrest, or use force on a person, except when race is part of the description of a specific suspect. The practice has a long history in police and minority relations. Nevertheless, prior to the events of September 11, there was a growing recognition, he said, that racial profiling was widespread, unconstitutional, and ineffective, as in the war on drugs. Since 9/11, however, this use of race has been combined with charges of minor violations as a pretext for police action and has been used increasingly by private and public security guards at malls and airports and by pilots acting in a law enforcement capacity.

There is another, less obvious, dimension to racial profiling—acts of omission; that is, police officers not responding appropriately when violations of civil rights occur. For example, police often do not take hate crimes seriously when they are reported by the victims or third-party observers.

In post-9/11 security and antiterrorism concerns, the objects of profiling are primarily Muslims, Arabs, and South Asians—rather than African Americans, Latinos, or other groups—but the tactics are the same. They are both unconstitutional and ineffective, alienating the very communities whose assistance is most needed for national security. Moreover, in the current post-9/11 climate, African

---

[1] Panelists' presentations were summarized from a transcript of the New York Advisory Committee's May 21, 2003, community forum in New York City. The transcript is on file with the Eastern Regional Office of the U.S. Commission on Civil Rights.

Americans and Latinos—communities traditionally hit hard by profiling—continue to suffer from intensified practices of racial profiling by law enforcement officials.

Khurrum Wahid, *Legal Advisor, Council on American-Islamic Relations*

Profiling by both local and federal law enforcement authorities is increasing, according to Mr. Wahid. In New York City, it shows up as selective enforcement. Police are citing young black men for "quality of life" violations, such as trespassing in Harlem housing projects or, in one instance, for sitting on a milk crate in front of one's own store. In addition, immigrant shopkeepers, mainly of Middle Eastern origin, have been subjected to selective and sudden enforcement of regulations requiring them to have a vending license—which may take up to 25 years to obtain—for what had been a long condoned practice of setting up tables in front of their stores.

The profiling of Muslims, Arabs, and South Asians by federal agencies is to be challenged for its ineffectiveness in increasing security. The use of watch lists—that is, lists of individual and organizational names designed to aid in the fight against terrorism—as the basis for federal law enforcement actions is a new issue as is the federal government's administrative powers to force private companies to practice racial and ethnic profiling on the government's behalf.

Muslims, Arabs, and South Asians are in constant fear of delays or denial of their right to travel because of the use of "no fly" lists and profiling by customs agents. A young man from the West Bank was flying to the United States as a student accepted in an MBA program. Meeting several other Palestinians in a stopover in Italy, they sat together for the last leg of their flight. Apparently, because they were conversing in Arabic, they were put in detention immediately upon arrival, held for 24 hours while enduring long questioning, and finally cleared and released by the Federal Bureau of Investigation (FBI)—only to be denied admission to the United States by INS (now in the DHS) and sent back to Italy. The practice of airline employees reporting "anything suspicious" to federal officials raises the issue of private company employees acting as agents of the government.

Financial targeting of Muslims, Arabs, and South Asians is another form of profiling in which the Office of Foreign Asset Control of the Department of Treasury has issued a list of several hundred names of persons who are blocked from financial transactions.[2] How one gets on the list, or challenges being on the list, and what safeguards exist against errors are unknown. One private company providing money transfer services seized $80 from a man whose name happens to be Muhammad Ali—a client of Mr. Wahid—because that very common name appeared on the blocked transaction list. Two private companies providing financial and banking services have dropped many of their customers and denied new accounts to other Muslim, Arab, and South Asian customers.

The encouragement by law enforcement agencies for the general public to provide anonymous tips relevant to antiterrorism security has led to thousands of useless tips based on profiling and many vindictive and retaliatory actions. Minor criminal infractions are being used as the reason to detain

---

[2] The 1990 Antiterrorism Act prohibits the provision of material support to a foreign terrorist organization. 18 U.S.C. § 2339b (2004). The Department of the Treasury may require U.S. financial institutions possessing or controlling assets of designated foreign terrorist organizations to block all financial transactions involving these assets. 18 U.S.C. §§ 1956, 1957 (2004). Executive Order 13,224, 66 Fed. Reg. 49,079 (2001) states that the Executive will freeze any assets which are used to assist in, sponsor, or provide financial, material, or technological support for, or financial or other services to or in support of, such acts of terrorism, or those persons listed in the Annex to the order, or determined to be subject to the order. The Treasury Department's Office of Foreign Assets Control coordinates efforts to freeze the assets of parties designated as terrorists. Once the terrorist designation has occurred, the group's or individual's name is published in the Federal Register. Upon designation, their assets are frozen immediately without prior notice of process.

Muslims, Arabs, and South Asians, holding them as long as possible with the presumption of terrorist ties or of knowledge of such as the basis for determining bail conditions. The immigration court has been doing this for 18 months, and it is now becoming common practice in federal criminal court and state family courts.

Bhairavi Desai, *Co-founder and Organizer, New York Taxi Drivers' Alliance*

Of the 100,000 licensed taxi drivers in New York City, 80 percent are immigrants. Sixty percent are South Asian—Bangladeshi, Pakistani, and Asian Indians—and 20 percent are Middle Eastern or West African. Seventy-five percent are Muslim or Sikh.

September 11 exacerbated drivers' already difficult economic situations. Furthermore, they have been the targets of hate crimes. After 9/11, three drivers' taxis, parked for the night at their residences, were set on fire. No one called the fire department. The owner of the taxi company subsequently sued one of those drivers for $3,000 for breach of contract.

There have been 10 incidents since 9/11 in which drivers have been pulled out of their cabs in broad daylight and punched and spat upon. No one came to assist them, including the police. In this climate, some wives are terrified and some parents kept their children at home for several weeks out of fear for their safety. Generally, people are not reporting these incidents. When complaints were filed with the NYPD, officials stated that their priority was antiterrorism.[3] The anti-immigrant, anti-Islamic bias of the now consolidated antiterrorism law enforcement agencies has trickled down to affect the behavior of ordinary people. When the police do not protect them, it encourages hate crimes.

The FBI has gone through the files of the Taxi and Limousine Commission for complaints and anonymous tips against South Asians, who have been called in and told to bring their immigration documentation and questioned with no attorney present. These anonymous tips often turn out to be retaliatory, such as by one owner who did not want a particular driver to leave his service.

Dennis D. Parker, *Bureau Chief, Civil Rights Bureau, Office of Eliot Spitzer, Attorney General of the State of New York*

Prior to 9/11, in 1999, the New York State Attorney General completed a study of the "stop and frisk" practices of the NYPD.[4] That study was done in the wake of rising concerns about the unfair targeting of African Americans and Latino Americans. While there are dramatic differences in the concerns of law enforcement after 9/11, the Attorney General's study identifies fundamental considerations and makes basic conclusions about the balance between the need to use particular law enforcement techniques in order to protect the public at large and the need to preserve the interests of individuals and particular communities.

---

[3] In a letter dated February 3, 2004, Stephen L. Hammerman, deputy commissioner of legal matters, New York City Police Department, wrote in response to these statements: "The Police Department protests the conclusory and unverified assertions so that these allegations may be investigated. The NYPD's mission is to investigate and prevent both conventional crime and terrorist acts, as evidenced by the fact that New York City is the safest large city in America."

[4] In a letter dated February 3, 2004, deputy commissioner of legal matters, New York City Police Department, wrote in response to this statement: "The NYPD continues to disagree with the Attorney General's conclusions and finds the study fatally flawed in failing to account for the factors which are relevant and necessary in assessing the Department's stop and frisk activity."

The study found that African Americans and Latinos were stopped at a higher rate than their proportion in the community—even after controlling for the crime rate in those populations and the neighborhoods in which they tend to reside. The study raised questions pertaining to factors such as training and supervision of law enforcement personnel, the efficacy of particular law enforcement techniques, and the need for balance in these interests. Effective policing and respect for individual rights are complementary. Civil rights without personal safety is a mirage; policing without respect for the rule of law is not policing at all.

The dramatically heightened need for increased security in the aftermath of 9/11—particularly the need to prevent future attacks—has affected the balance between security and the civil rights and liberties of citizens. With regard to those matters within the Attorney General's authority, the office has taken steps to ensure the safety of New Yorkers without unduly burdening the rights of individuals. These steps included a careful examination of existing New York statutes to determine if that law was sufficient to respond to the specific threats of what had been previously unimagined acts of terrorism. As a result of that examination, the Office of the Attorney General supported and presented a legislative package that clarified the penal law to ease the apprehension and prosecution of persons charged with terrorist attacks and to ensure that the punishment is commensurate with the gravity of the offenses.[5] Moreover, state law enforcement officials have sought to cooperate with federal officials in the prevention of terrorist acts in a manner that does not interfere with their legal responsibilities and obligations under state law.

Of all the factors that would be useful in considering federal antiterrorism policies, most important is the realization that the effectiveness of a particular law enforcement policy is only a part of the calculus that must be undertaken—there must also be the realization that there is the potential for costs for the implementation of the policy. These costs can include the targeting of individuals, not for their behavior but for who and what they are, a practice that has potential implications for their ability to enjoy the benefits of American citizenship, the very benefits which are most under attack by terrorists. In evaluating specific security measures, particularly those that would affect a discrete segment of American society, it is vital that there be a realistic assessment of the threat to the American people, some consideration of the consequences of a failure to take the step, an examination of alternative, less intrusive means of achieving goals, and a careful consideration of the effect on the rights of individuals.

Nicolas Rossier, *Film Director, Baraka Productions*

A 10-minute segment of Mr. Rossier's documentary, *Brothers and Others*, was shown, depicting the effects on an Arab American family in which the father was arrested, presumably for visa violations, leaving the devastated wife and four children embarrassed and frightened, yet determined to speak up against this injustice. Other accounts of intimidating questioning and detention were documented, as well as statements presented by intellectual and religious spokespersons, who decried the "moral hypocrisy" of their treatment and the ineffectiveness of profiling as a tool in making the United States more secure.

---

[5] A bill reflecting key points presented in this legislative package passed in the New York State Senate on February 11, 2003. As of February 25, 2004, however, this bill had not been introduced into the New York State Assembly. State legislators in support of the antiterrorism package argue its necessity to better prevent terrorist acts in the future. Opponents of the legislation are concerned about potential abuses on the civil liberties of domestic criminal defendants and argue that such legislation is already in place at the federal level. *See* Joel Stashenko, "Anti-Terrorism Package Has Not Been Passed, Despite Shock of Sept. 11," *Associated Press State and Local News Wire*, Sept. 6, 2003.

Regardless of whether the viewer accepts the film as an objective report of the plight of Muslim and Arab communities in the New York area, Mr. Rossier said, at a minimum the film evidences the nature of the discussion, and extent of the discontent, within Muslim and Arab communities regarding the practices that immigration and law enforcement agencies have targeted against them.

Panel 2: Border Crossing and Special Registration Issues

Community relations with law enforcement agencies took on new dimensions in the wake of 9/11. Two areas in which there were dramatic changes are with respect to border crossings and the registration of nonimmigrants. After 9/11, the U.S. government initiated the National Security Entry/Exit Registration System (NSEERS). The first phase of this system was implemented on September 11, 2002. It required selected individuals to be fingerprinted, photographed, and interviewed under oath at U.S. ports of entry. On November 6, 2002, the NSEERS program was expanded to require noncitizens from certain countries already in the United States on nonimmigrant visas to register at local INS offices.[6] This second phase, referred to as Call-In Special Registration, required males over the age of 16 from a list of 25 countries to visit INS offices, be fingerprinted, photographed, and questioned by an inspection officer. With the exception of North Korea, all countries on the list are predominantly Muslim.

After special registration requirements were announced and the first phase of the program implemented, many Muslim families attempted to flee the United States, crossing the border into Canada to seek asylum status. DHS policies are alleged to have changed at different locations along the U.S.-Canadian border with respect to the arrest and detention of those attempting to cross the Canadian border or those sent back by the Canadian authorities.

The New York Advisory Committee selected Panel 2 speakers to examine the civil rights concerns of those subjected to special registration requirements and of those seeking asylum in Canada, as well as the interconnection between the U.S. Call-In Special Registration program and the reports of increased flight to Canada by noncitizen Muslims living in the United States. Specifically, the Committee sought information on how the implementation of the DHS policies and the requirements for the Call-In Special Registration may have affected the civil rights of immigrants.

In New York City, noncitizens required to undergo special registration initially reported to the 3rd floor of the Jacob Javits Federal Building. Noncitizens whose immigration status was unclear or who were out of status were referred to the 10th floor of this building, which housed DHS' immigration investigations unit.

Border Crossing

Elizabeth Woike, *Acting Executive Director, Vive, Inc., Buffalo, New York*

Vive, Inc., provides food, shelter, medical care, and legal advice to Canadian-bound asylum seekers. Vive makes appointments for refugee claimants at the Canadian border. When people come to Vive to seek asylum in Canada, Vive faxes the names and general information to Citizenship and Immigration Canada (CIC), which then makes an appointment for the person. At the time of the appointment at the border, the person undergoes a full background check and is fingerprinted and photo-

---

[6] Four country listings were identified in separate Federal Register publications. The final Call-In Special Registration period ended on April 25, 2003. Registration through NSEERS continues at U.S. ports of entry.

graphed. If the person is determined to be eligible, the person is allowed into Canada to pursue his or her asylum claim.

Ms. Woike reported that Vive served 6,174 people from March 2002 to April 2003—the most ever served over a comparable period in the 19-year history of the organization. Vive normally serves between 4,000 and 5,000 people annually. Ms. Woike described how the increase in the numbers of people Vive served from December 2002 until April 2003 was directly linked to special registration, supporting her conclusion with office statistics and what the people served told Vive staff. After the government announced the countries in Group 3 whose nationals had to report for special registration in mid-December 2002 (Pakistan and Saudi Arabia),[7] the number of asylum seekers from Pakistan increased to 156 for that month, compared with 11 for the previous month. Moreover, the number of people needing Vive's services increased in ensuing months. In February 2003, for example, Vive served 959 persons. Of this number, 513 were Pakistani nationals.

CIC was overwhelmed by the increased number of asylum seekers. It usually takes between four and seven days to obtain an appointment with CIC to apply for asylum. With the overflow of people, it took an average of five to seven weeks to get an appointment. At one point in February and early March 2003, there were more than 800 people waiting for appointments with CIC at the Buffalo border. With Vive full to capacity, the overflow stayed at local hotels and some went back to New York City to wait for their appointments. Others tried crossing the border at Plattsburg, New York.

The Pakistani population served by Vive ranged from people who had been in the United States for several years to others who arrived more recently. They were single men and many family groups with woman and children, both U.S.-born and undocumented children. Sixty-four U.S.-born children of Pakistani parents passed through Vive in February 2003. Once people realized that it would take between five and seven weeks to get an appointment with CIC—which would have prevented many of them from leaving the United States before the final Call-In Special Registration deadline for Pakistani nationals—the number of Pakistanis dropped off in March to 156 and again to 45 in April.

With the federal government's announcement of Group 4 for special registration (Bangladesh, Egypt, Indonesia, Jordan, and Kuwait),[8] Vive received an increased number of nationals from those countries. In March 2003, Vive served 52 Egyptians and, in April 2003, 127 Bangladeshis and 12 Indonesians.

At the end of January 2003, CIC began doing "direct backs"; that is, sending people who arrived at the border without an appointment back to the United States. Anyone who was directed back to the United States and out of legal immigration status was placed in removal proceedings. Some were detained by INS. At the Buffalo border, this seldom happened because most of the people came through Vive first, where they could stay while awaiting their appointment. As for outbound checks—people who were checked by U.S. immigration leaving the United States going into Canada—Ms. Woike testified that she was aware of two incidents. In those incidents the people were not detained.

Lastly, Ms. Woike addressed the Safe Third Country Agreement between the United States and Canada, part of the Smart Border 30-point plan.[9] Signed on December 5, 2002, it has not been imple-

---

[7] Registration and Monitoring of Certain Non-immigrants, 67 Fed. Reg. 77,642–44 (2003); 68 Fed. Reg. 8,046–47 (2003).

[8] Registration and Monitoring of Certain Non-immigrants, 68 Fed. Reg. 2,363–66 (2003); 68 Fed. Reg. 8,046–47 (2003).

[9] On December 3, 2001, Attorney General John Ashcroft signed an accord with the minister of citizenship and immigration of Canada and the solicitor general of Canada agreeing to begin discussions on a safe third country exception to the right to apply for asylum. The *Agreement Between the Government of Canada and the Government of the United States of America for Cooperation in the Examination of Refugee Status Claims from Nationals of Third Countries* was signed in

mented yet.[10] Under the agreement, those who arrived first in the United States must apply in the United States for asylum; they will not be able to make a refugee claim in Canada except under limited exceptions. Ms. Woike testified to the expected rush at the border before the agreement is implemented, and she predicts it will be worse than during special registration. After the Safe Third Country Agreement is implemented, there will be concerns about border security. Since the agreement only prevents people arriving at the Canadian border from the United States from making asylum claims in Canada, people who make it inland to the interior of Canada can still bring asylum claims. This may encourage and escalate smuggling into Canada and raise a host of security concerns.[11]

Patrick Giantonio, *Executive Director, Vermont Refugee Assistance*

Initially, Vermont Refugee Assistance worked primarily with Canadian-bound asylum seekers. Since 1993, it broadened its services to include immigrant detainees in county jails in Vermont and upstate New York. It does not have a shelter, but rather houses asylum seekers in the community. It focuses on those seeking to file asylum at two ports of entry: the Champlain-Lacole, New York-Quebec border and the Vermont-Quebec border.

Mr. Giantonio testified that special registration was highly discriminatory, wrong, unjust, and illegal. He described the surge in numbers of people attempting to file for political asylum at the Champlain border in Quebec as a response to special registration and changing U.S. and Canadian policies. Because of the evolving Canadian immigration policy and the need to manage the flow of asylum seekers from the United States, Quebec Immigration and CIC consolidated their resources at the Champlain-Lacole port of entry, virtually closing the Vermont border port of entry to asylum applicants. Normally, asylum applicants would arrive at Champlain, go right by the DHS, and present themselves to Canadian officials. They would have their initial interview and be paroled into Canada. It had been a longstanding policy of CIC for officials at a port of entry who wanted to return someone with an appointment to the United States for them to first obtain assurances from INS that the individual would be able to make it back to Canada for their appointment. In other words, Canada immigration did not want to return people to the United States if they would be placed in detention.

However, as the number of people seeking asylum increased, on January 27, 2003, CIC changed its policy—if CIC wanted to send someone with an appointment back to the United States, it did not

---

2002, but does not go into effect until September of 2004. For text, see Citizen and Immigration Canada, "Canada and U.S. Negotiators Agree to Final Draft Text of Safe Third Country Agreement," <http://www.cic.gc.ca/english/policy/safe-third.html> (last accessed Feb. 18, 2004). The agreement provides, with four exceptions, that asylum seekers who arrive at a port of entry along the Canada-U.S. land border will be obliged to seek protection in the first country of arrival. In other words, asylum seekers on the U.S. side of the border attempting entry into Canada will be deflected back to the United States and vice versa.

[10] As of February 10, 2004, the agreement remained to be implemented.

[11] In a letter dated January 20, 2004, Jason P. Ahern, assistant commissioner, Office of Field Operations, U.S. Customs and Border Protection, Department of Homeland Security, wrote that this written testimony addresses "actions taken by border agencies, both Canadian and U.S., in response to the surge in asylum applicants traveling to Canada, many of whom were out of legal immigration status in the United States. Federal authorities have a responsibility to enforce the laws of the United States and to take appropriate action when they encounter violators, and Federal agencies must often adjust their enforcement procedures and tactics in response to emergencies and trends as they occur. The Immigration and Naturalization Service (INS) and later CBP worked closely with Citizenship and Immigration Canada (CIC) and with the advocacy organizations to manage this influx as efficiently as possible in accordance with existing laws, regulations and policies. What is not reflected in the testimony is how INS worked with the Salvation Army in Plattsburg and Vermont Refugee Assistance (VRA) to arrange pick up service for women and children, assisted in obtaining food for applicants who had been waiting for many hours while being processed in Canada, set up special processing areas in the port of entry to deal with these cases as quickly as possible, and avoided the use of hold rooms whenever possible."

have to seek assurance from INS that the individual would not be placed in detention. The total number of asylum seekers returned from Champlain to the United States was 432, of whom 133 were to be detained if they did not post a bond. As of March 5, 2003, 63 people were detained.

Under Canadian immigration law, people can still make a claim for asylum in Canada even when their case had been denied in the United States. Those individuals who were sent back by Canada to the United States and subsequently detained and deported because they had prior orders of removal in the United States were effectively denied the protection of and access to the Canadian system. With the crisis at the border, asylum seekers ended up straddling two immigration systems. They started the asylum process in Canada and if they were sent back to the United States and detained, they had to resolve their immigration removal proceedings in the United States. Mr. Giantonio stressed that the process to which Canadian-bound asylum seekers were subjected was inefficient and contended that most U.S. officials working at the border agree.

At the height of the crisis, the INS and the Bureau of Customs and Border Protection (BCBP) began outbound checks. Some asylum seekers en route to the Champlain border were caught in the outbound checks. Because of Vermont Refugee Assistance's great working relationship with local law enforcement authorities, the DHS port director agreed if someone had an appointment with Canadian immigration, that person would be allowed to continue to Canada even if he or she was out of status. Mr. Giantonio testified that it was difficult for detainees to access attorneys. Bonds were typically set by INS officials at $1,500 initially, but then jumped to $5,000 across the board.[12]

Bobby Khan, *Outreach Coordinator, Coney Island Avenue Project*

The Coney Island Avenue Project was formed in the immediate aftermath of 9/11 to deal with the effect of post-9/11 government policies directed at the Pakistani community. Mr. Khan detailed the human toll that such policies left in their wake in the Pakistani community. He framed the human toll as taking place in two phases. First, in the immediate aftermath of 9/11, law enforcement authorities made raids on the Pakistani community, going door to door and making arrests of scores of Pakistani male immigrants. He described the case of one Pakistani man who was held as a material witness and died in prison after languishing there for six weeks. The Coney Island Avenue Project demanded an investigation into his death, but never received any information that such an investigation had been carried out. Another Pakistani man was arrested right after 9/11 for overstaying his visa. He was kept with 25 other Pakistanis on the 9th floor at the Metropolitan Detention Center, where they were reportedly beaten every day.[13]

---

[12] In a letter dated January 20, 2004, Jason P. Ahern, assistant commissioner, Office of Field Operations, U.S. Customs and Border Protection, Department of Homeland Security, wrote in response to this statement: "We believe this is an inaccurate characterization. Only in very rare cases were bonds of over $5,000 imposed and in many cases, the individuals were released without bond. The INS took into consideration both mitigating and negative factors in determining whether to impose a bond and at what amount, including equity in the United States, whether there were children involved, the seriousness of the immigration violation, the length of overstay, whether the alien had a criminal record, and other such circumstances. We also note that there were indications that both CIC and INS experienced substantial no-show rates for hearings."

[13] In a letter dated February 4, 2004, Michael W. Garrett, senior deputy assistant director, Federal Bureau of Prisons, U.S. Department of Justice, wrote in response to these allegations: "The Department of Justice does not condone the abuse of anyone being held in federal custody. Additionally, the Department, through its Civil Rights Division, aggressively prosecutes state and federal officers who violate the rights of those in custody. Since September 11, 2001, the Department, working with the Federal Bureau of Investigation and United States Attorneys' offices, has investigated allegations regarding 19 Arab, South Asian, and Muslim federal detainees, which raise complaints that the detainees were physically assaulted by law enforcement officers while in custody. All 19 allegations presented insufficient evidence to support a fed-

After this first phase of arrests, there was the second phase—special registration. As a result of the fear of special registration, almost 20,000 Pakistanis have migrated to Canada, according to Mr. Khan.

Mr. Khan spoke of families transporting infant children across the border in chilling winter weather. He detailed the plight of another Pakistani family that was directed back to the United States by CIC. The husband was arrested and detained by U.S. authorities. Mr. Khan described how bonds jump from $1,500 to $15,000[14]—a move he termed "highway robbery."

Of those who opted to report to special registration, many were kept at the registration site for 30 hours without any food or drink. If they were taken to investigations, some were ordered to take off their clothes, shackled, and ultimately sent to prison. Others were given notices to appear and placed in removal proceedings.

Winston Barrus, *Interim Deputy Director, Buffalo Field Office, Bureau of Customs and Border Protection (BCBP), U.S. Department of Homeland Security*

Mr. Barrus gave an overview of the role and responsibilities of the Bureau of Customs and Border Protection within the Department of Homeland Security. BCBP is now the agency with jurisdiction and authority to enforce the inspection provisions of the Immigration and Nationality Act.[15] The Buffalo Field Office of BCBP has jurisdiction over the state of New York outside metropolitan New York City. This includes all New York-Canada ports of entry from the Peace Bridge in Buffalo to the inspection station at Rouses Point.

Mr. Barrus explained the inspection requirements at the port of entry for persons seeking entry into the United States. To be admissible as a nonimmigrant, people are generally required to be in possession of a valid passport and visa and establish that they have a residence abroad to which they intend to return. Each year, BCBP conducts approximately 500 million inspections of applicants for admission into the United States. Most applicants are nonimmigrants who depart after their authorized stay has expired. Others overstay their authorized stay, some attempt to enter with fraudulent documents, and some enter without being inspected. If immigration authorities encounter these individuals, they are subject to removal proceedings.

Recently, large numbers of Pakistani nationals have been appearing at Canadian land border ports of entry seeking to apply for Canadian refugee status. The increase in Pakistani nationals seeking to apply for Canadian refugee status may have been precipitated by NSEERS. Nonimmigrants seeking to apply for Canadian refugee status should do so when they have a lawful U.S. status. Nonimmigrants who are refused admission into Canada and have a lawful U.S. status are allowed to proceed back into the United States with no further action taken. Nonimmigrants who are refused admission into Canada and have an unlawful U.S. status are processed at the port of entry as removable aliens.

---

eral criminal prosecution for the willful violation of any detainee's constitutionally protected rights. With one exception, all of the 19 matters investigated as possible federal criminal violations involved no serious injury to the victim. In some cases, investigators were unable to corroborate that there had been any injury at all."

[14] *See* footnote 12, chapter 2.

[15] The Homeland Security Act of 2002, Pub. L. No. 107-296, 116 Stat. 2135 (2002), transferred the functions of the INS to the DHS. Under the act, the INS was to be abolished and its functions transferred from the Department of Justice to the DHS, effective March 1, 2003. According to the Reorganization Plan Modification for the Department of Homeland Security, the U.S. Customs Service has been renamed to the Bureau of Customs and Border Protection. H.R. Doc. No. 108-32 at 4 (2003).

With its authority to make custody and bond determinations, BCBP makes these determinations on a case-by-case basis.

Following 9/11, the federal government established outbound inspections at certain ports of entry to Canada, including Peace Bridge and Champlain. If inspectors encounter someone during an outbound check who is not a U.S. citizen and does not appear to have proper travel documents, that person is referred for further inspection. The fact that some of the nonimmigrants who BCBP encounters are seeking to depart the United States or may be intending to apply for Canadian refugee status does not affect BCBP's requirement to process them for removal under the immigration laws if they are illegally in the country.

Since 9/11, BCBP has received significant increases in staffing and technology at ports of entry in an effort to prevent terrorists or weapons of mass destruction from entering the country. BCBP's duties are now performed with increased vigilance and attention to detail regarding all applicants for admission into the United States. On April 29, 2003, it was announced that DHS will create a new entry/exit system backed by 21st century technology.[16] The U.S. Visitor and Immigrant Status system (U.S. Visit) is designed to make entering the United States easier for legitimate tourists, students, and business travelers, while making it more difficult to enter the United States illegally, through the implementation of biometrically authenticated documents such as photographs, fingerprints, or iris scans.

Special Registration

Mohammad Sarfaraz Hussain, *High School Student*

Young Mohammad Sarfaraz Hussain was required to comply with special registration with Group 3 nationals. On the day of the SAC forum, he was in school. However, he submitted a handwritten letter addressed to the New York Advisory Committee (text set out below), which was read into the record.

> Sorry I am not here in person, I'm in school. However, I would like for you to please read this out loud. First I would like to thank District Director Edward McElroy for letting me stay in the U.S. I am very thankful. I ask you please to tell Washington leaders not to make the States have the special registration program again. The process was very long. I missed a whole day of school. I waited in the cold for about 3½ hours just to get in the building. I didn't know what was going on. I had questions in my head, why am I here? I learned about special registration from my uncle. Otherwise, I would be going on with my everyday life. After I got in the building, I saw many Muslim people in there. Some were scared to death; some were very upset and angry. For me I was thinking when am I going to get out of here? I got a basketball game tomorrow and school. All that kinda changed when I was asked to go to the 10th floor investigation and my lawyer wasn't allowed to stay with me. I was scared, but they treated me well because my lawyer made a fuss about sending a teenager to the 10th floor without an attorney. The person who interviewed me didn't mix me up with the general population and

---

[16] The integrated automated entry/exit system will verify the identities of foreign nationals and authenticate their travel documents through the comparison of biometric identifiers. The Department of Homeland Security will take a digital photograph and two fingerprints from each nonimmigrant alien who presents a visa at designated air or sea ports of entry. The inspecting officer will be able to compare the biometrics associated with the person who applied for the visa at the consular office abroad against the biometrics of the person that is present at the port of entry. Nonimmigrant visa holders, except those subject to the National Security Entry/Exit Registration System (NSEERS), may continue to depart through any port, even though biometrics are not currently being collected on exit. Individuals who remain subject to NSEERS must still depart through specific ports and undergo special departure procedures. 8 U.S.C. §§ 1187, 1365a, and note, 1379, 1731–31 (2004); Implementation of the United States Visitor and Immigrant Status Indicator Technology System (US-VISIT); Biometric Requirements, 69 Fed. Reg. 468 (2004).

didn't put much pressure on me. He did ask me questions, like if I belonged to any groups. And if I wanted to file for political asylum when he asked if I would like to let the Pakistani consulate know about me. I was scared and did not know how to answer that question. The interviewer said he would ask my attorney that question. I did see people being asked questions they had no idea or clue of, like they were criminals.

Then it kinda hit me and I felt very lost in this world at that moment. I don't think anybody would like to feel that experience. It is sad that natives from Muslim countries had to register. Because it wasn't their fault that they were born in Muslim countries. And now they are being penalized for being human "with a different faith and geography." After all, Muslims breathe, eat, drink water like any other human being. If they were real terrorists, they wouldn't go and register. I know people who were there at special registration with me who are being deported. I don't think they should be, because they obeyed the law by showing up and other natives from different countries that were not Muslims did not have to register. I got to Immigration at 8:00 in the morning and finished at 11:00 at night. I know I'm lucky because I still kinda think what would have happen to me if I were sent back to Pakistan, the home I never knew.

Yours truly, Mohammad Sarfaraz Hussain, May, 19, 2003

Karin Anderson, *Policy and Training Associate, New York Immigration Coalition*

The New York Immigration Coalition is an umbrella policy and advocacy organization for more than 150 member groups in New York that work with immigrants and refugees. It coordinated the Special Registration Legal Assistance Project, a collaborative effort by community organizations and legal services groups. The project has assisted more than 800 individuals through legal clinics offering advice for those subject to special registration requirements.

Ms. Anderson described how the special registration program suffered from fundamental flaws in its design, the most serious of which was its use of nationality-based profiling to determine who must register, ignoring data that show broad-based profiling methods that target persons based on characteristics such as race or nationality are ineffective law enforcement tools. According to the Bureau of Citizenship and Immigration Services (BCIS), the number of people charged with terrorism-related crimes as a result of special registration is zero. Secondly, the design of the program did not give any consideration to the problems inherent in trying to implement such a large-scale enforcement program, especially in light of limited agency resources.

There was insufficient staffing and other resources needed to timely process the large number of registrants. Immigration adjudication officers had to be pulled away from their normal duties and diverted to help deal with special registration. As a consequence, the processing of immigration applications suffered tremendously, adding to an already formidable backlog of cases.

Ms. Anderson highlighted the implementation problems at the special registration site in New York City:

- *Lack of public notice:* Call-in registration was announced initially only through the Federal Register and later on the INS/BCIS Web site.[17] However, only those with Internet access, versed in written English, and with knowledge of the requirement knew to click on the special registration link to learn more. Moreover, the information on the Web site

---

[17] The Department of Justice says that publication in the Federal Register unequivocally constitutes sufficient notice for due process purposes. *See* 44 U.S.C. § 1507 (2003). The courts have held that publication in the Federal Register constitutes adequate due notice. *See* Lyng v. Payne, 476 U.S. 926, 942–43 (1986).

link was incorrect and confusing. For example, the Arabic notice for Group 2 incorrectly stated only those entering *after* September 30, 2002, were required to register. Later the Group 4 extension notice gave confusing information about who was required to register. Subsequently, as a result of these errors, the Group 2 deadline was extended and INS had to clarify the Group 4 requirements.

- *Lack of interpreters:* INS/BCIS did not provide interpreters on the 3rd floor, and the quality of interpreters on the 10th floor was unreliable, though the director of the New York office stated that they would be available. This was particularly problematic since the program required testimony under oath. Instead of professional interpreters, immigration officers relied on volunteer interpreters, family members, or friends of registrants, or even complete strangers to interpret for registrants. Officers called in the crowd, "Anybody speak Arabic, Urdu, etc?" Some officers denied the registrant an interpreter if they felt the registrant's English was "good enough." The result was that limited- or non-English-speaking registrants were forced to register even though they did not understand what was happening.

- *Denial of attorney access:* Registrants were denied access to their attorneys at the investigations unit, the place where they were the most vulnerable. DHS' Bureau of Immigration and Customs Enforcement officials initially stated that registrants would have access to their attorneys throughout the registration process. The bureau subsequently explained that attorneys would only be allowed to be present at investigations if their clients were making sworn statements. Denial of attorney access had disastrous consequences for some immigrants. For example, one young man referred to the investigations unit was denied access to his attorney. He mistakenly waived his right to a hearing. As a result, he was detained pending deportation.

- *Conditions of detention:* On the 10th floor, some people spent as long as 36 hours at special registration, in a large holding cell. Some registrants were handcuffed. The officers on the 10th floor acted in an intimidating manner. Registrants reported they were treated like criminals and were searched in a demeaning manner. There were some interpreters on the 10th floor, but some registrants reported that they were not competent.

- *Lack of training and oversight of interviewing officers:* This resulted in varying outcomes for similarly situated individuals. Some were registered and released; others were referred to the investigations unit and placed in removal proceedings. For example, some officers registered individuals who last entered the United States on Special Agricultural Worker visas, while others refused to do so. In some cases, individuals who claimed to have last entered the United States with nonimmigrant visas but who subsequently lost their documents were allowed to register, while others were refused.

- *Atmosphere of intimidation:* The attitude and behavior of many officers toward registrants created an atmosphere of fear in the unit and prevented registrants from asserting their rights. Officers were often impatient with limited- or non-English-speaking registrants, pressuring them to be interviewed even when they repeatedly stated they did not understand. In several cases, registrants wept openly as officers taunted them. People were not allowed to leave even under emergency conditions; that is, to get milk for a young child who accompanied his father to special registration. On several occasions, individuals waiting to register witnessed other registrants being handcuffed and removed from the room. Family members of registrants referred to the 10th floor investigations unit sat waiting for hours for their relatives to return, without any explanation as to what was happening and when or whether the registrant would return.

- *Lack of guidance from headquarters to the New York District Office:* In several cases of inconsistency, confusion was caused by lack of guidance from headquarters on how to deal with certain situations. For example, many would-be registrants who had lost their documents were turned away, but were not given any proof that they had tried to register. Such individuals could later be accused of not complying with the registration require- ment, and could be subject to criminal penalties and be deportable as a result.

Cyrus Mehta, *Chair, Committee on Immigration and Nationality Law of the Association of the Bar of the City of New York; First Vice Chair, Board of Trustees of the American Immigration Law Foundation*

Mr. Mehta testified to the comparisons between government initiatives targeting Japanese Americans during World War II because of their ancestry, without regard to individualized guilt or suspicion and present-day government initiatives targeting noncitizens from predominantly Muslim countries based on their nationality and gender without regard to individualized guilt or suspicion. No reports have been received of terrorists being prosecuted criminally as a result of the mass registration of Muslims.

Because they responded to the call to register, many are in deportation proceedings. Most affected are male teenagers who may have come to the United States as young children with their parents, totally unable to control their ability to remain in the United States legally. Registrants were routinely denied the right to counsel if they were sent to investigations. In New York City, this occurred regu- larly, even after the district director said that attorneys must be allowed access. Qualified translators were also not permitted to accompany registrants to investigations.

Mr. Mehta also focused on the ongoing requirements of special registration. Registration at the air- port or through the call-in program is not a one-time event. This person will constantly be branded as a "registered alien," as he will need to report back to INS on a periodic basis and exit the country only through certain designated ports of entry. Any failure to comply with all the requirements of this program (which also includes a duty to report a change of address) can lead to deportation, criminal penalties, and future inadmissibility.[18]

Mr. Mehta noted that INS used unapproved paper forms that failed to comply with the public protec- tion provisions of Section 3512 of the Paper Work Reduction Act to register people.[19] Form I-877, for example, stipulates that the statement "must be given freely and voluntarily." However, the final registration rule makes clear that any willful failure or refusal to comply with the required informa- tion collection would constitute a failure to maintain nonimmigrant status and a deportable offense.

---

[18] The Attorney General has authority to establish conditions of admission under 8 U.S.C. § 1184 (2004), and also promul- gate regulations for the registration, reporting of changes of address, and special registration of nonimmigrants under 8 U.S.C. §§ 1303, 1305 (2004). For regulations on registration and monitoring of certain nonimmigrants, see 8 C.F.R. parts 214 and 264 (2004).

[19] Under pre-August 2002 regulations at 8 C.F.R. § 264.1(a), the Immigration and Naturalization Service registers nonim- migrants using Form I-94 (Arrival-Departure Record). As authorized by 8 U.S.C. § 1302(c), the INS regulations at 8 C.F.R. § 264.1(e) contain general provisions waiving the fingerprinting requirements for many nonimmigrants.

Mr. Mehta presented the findings of a survey entitled "Inconsistency, Confusion and Chaos: Experiences with Call-In Special Registration" conducted by the American Immigration Law Foundation on registrants' experiences at Call-In Special Registration. The findings, based on 266 responses, were grouped into the following categories that illustrate the inconsistency and lack of clarity of the program's implementation:

- *Differential treatment with in-status nonimmigrants:* Some registrants were treated courteously, while others were asked intrusive questions and subjected to rude officers. Many had to wait long hours to register. In the experience of Mr. Mehta's firm, simple cases could take eight hours, and complicated cases took from 12 to 15 hours. Many of those assigned to register people at INS lacked basic knowledge of immigration laws and procedures.

- *Late registrants:* Of the late registrants, some were registered, others were put into removal proceedings, and two were arrested and incarcerated in county jails. Mr. Mehta witnessed needlessly harsh treatment of registrants. Some registrants should not have been placed in removal proceedings.

- *Registrants with applications for Lawful Permanent Residency:* There was inconsistency in the treatment of registrants with applications for Lawful Permanent Residency. Of those registrants whose nonimmigrant visas had expired, but who had filed an application for adjustment of status, some were allowed to continue to pursue the applications after registering, while others were placed in removal proceedings.

- *Dual citizenship:* No clarity was provided as to how to deal with dual citizenship. It was uncertain whether someone who was born in a targeted country but a citizen of another, non-targeted country automatically had to register.

- *Credit cards:* It was unclear why people were asked to provide INS their credit or debit card numbers.

Omar T. Mohammedi, *President, New York Area Muslim Bar Association*

Mr. Mohammedi's testimony focused on the shortcomings of special registration under the National Security Entry/Exit Registration System. He contended that the program has been administered without a clear vision or consistent policy and that it is an ad hoc, misleading solution to a real problem. Special registration will not enhance national security because it targets innocent people based on their race, national origin, and religion, rather than terrorists.

The addition and subsequent removal of Armenia from the list of countries raises even more questions about the criteria and process by which countries are included in the list. People who come forward to identify themselves under this program are seeking to obey the law; a terrorist would not report to INS. The hardworking families coming forward to register do not have criminal records; they pay taxes and contribute to the development and wealth of this country. Yet, many of those who complied with the program by registering have been detained, deported, or are awaiting deportation due to immigration technicalities resulting from INS bureaucracies and backlogs in issuing green cards.

Registrants have been denied attorney representation, interrogated with their hands cuffed, and subjected to verbal abuse. Those taken in custody were placed in handcuffs and leg shackles and held in cold cells without adequate clothing or blankets. Some were forced to sleep standing up or on concrete floors because of overcrowding.

Moreover, many who complied with special registration may have well-founded fears of persecution, but may not have filed timely asylum applications. Under Article 3 of the International Convention Against Torture, the U.S. government has an obligation not to return refugees to persecution.[20]

Mr. Mohammedi reported incidents of people who were in status and complied with special registration requirements, but who suffered nonetheless from inconsistent procedures at the INS. Registrants with international travel plans, for example, were told they must provide notice of departure to the INS agent before leaving the United States. In some instances, husbands of families who had to travel outside the United States and who attempted to report to INS found no immigration officer available. These men were told that they could depart and that they just needed to explain their situation upon their return; that is, that there was no immigration officer available to fill out the report prior to departure. However, when returning, these men were barred from reentering the United States. These people had their careers, families, and future here, but are inadmissible now because INS failed to implement the registration program effectively. Mr. Mohammedi played tapes of two families describing their plight. The families now face deportation as a result of complying with special registration.

Panel 3: Legal Issues After 9/11: Due Process, Checks and Balances, and Access to Public Records

The third panel picked up on the topics of racial profiling and special registration and border crossing issues, and presented them in the context of the adequacy of protections for civil rights and civil liberties. Panelists addressed concerns about the sufficiency of due process in current law enforcement practices, particularly in the administration of immigration law as it affects Muslims, Arabs, and South Asians. In addition, the third panel included a presentation of new privacy and records access issues that have arisen since September 11, which bear directly on the ability to ensure independent oversight of civil rights concerns in law enforcement activities.

Rebecca Thornton, *Fellow, Lawyers Committee for Human Rights*

Ms. Thornton contended that many of the measures taken by government since September 11 have violated traditional notions of liberty with no clear connection to increased safety. Checks and balances designed into the American constitutional system have been eviscerated by the Departments of Justice and the Office (now Department) of Homeland Security, so that there are now few effective checks on arbitrary, irrational, destructive, or even malicious behavior by the tens of thousands of people who enforce immigration law.

Her remarks focused on the erosion of due process represented by denial of individualized hearings, expanded authority to detain without charge, barriers to release on bond, and prolonged detention after final deportation orders have been issued. She also addressed discriminatory policies in the in-

---

[20] "No State Party shall expel, return ('refouler') or extradite a person to another state where there are substantial grounds for believing that he would be in danger of being subjected to torture. For the purpose of determining whether there are such grounds, the competent authorities shall take into account all relevant considerations including, where applicable, the existence in the state concerned of a consistent pattern of gross, flagrant or mass violations of human rights." The International Convention Against Torture and Other Cruel, Inhuman or Degrading Treatment or Punishment, Dec. 10, 1984, S. Treaty Doc. No. 100-20 (1988), 1465 U.N.T.S. 85.

terview process, selective enforcement of immigration law, and special registration requirements that have been targeted at particular communities of Muslim and Middle Eastern foreign nationals. As a result, people in these minority communities, citizens and noncitizens alike, feel under siege.

According to Ms. Thornton, one cannot say whether any benefits to national security have resulted from these increased security shortcuts, or whether more traditional standards of due process and fair procedure would have been any less effective than these recently adopted practices. It is clear, however, that an opportunity has been lost to determine whether national security could have been enhanced through increased cooperation from the affected communities, simply by treating those communities equally and more fairly.

David Harris, *Balk Professor of Law and Values, University of Toledo College of Law; Soros Senior Justice Fellow, Open Society Institute of New York*

Mr. Harris described his findings that racial profiling is inefficient and diverts time and attention from much more effective methods of police work. Based on statistics collected by state agencies, he found that the "hit rate," which is the rate at which police stops of individuals result in arrests or finding contraband, is actually lower for the minority groups being profiled as more likely to commit crimes than it is for whites, who are not being profiled.

Mr. Harris stated his belief that his conclusions with respect to racial and ethnic profiling generally were equally true of the focus on Muslims and Middle Easterners in the aftermath of September 11. Good police work is based on observation of suspicious behavior, not appearance. Profiles of personal characteristics such as race, faith, or national origin actually reduce, not enhance, the ability of law enforcement to catch wrongdoers. Those personal characteristics are what Mr. Harris calls distracters. They divert attention from the very behaviors that are the basis of good police work.

In addition, profiling for race, faith, or national origin has the effect of enlarging the suspect pool. As a result, profiling forces departments to spend their resources unproductively, addressing cases that have nothing to them—a pattern that has been evident since September 11.

Mr. Harris' third point is that not only does the best intelligence come from talking to people, but doing so has never been more critical. More information and informants are needed now. Useful information on terrorist activity involving Middle Easterners must come from Middle Eastern communities. But profiling those same people drives willing informants away by sowing fear and distrust.

Arthur N. Eisenberg, *Legal Director, New York Civil Liberties Union*

Mr. Eisenberg addressed the reduction in accountability for official misbehavior brought about by changes since September 11, focusing on changes to the consent decree in *Handschu v. Special Services Division*.[21] He explained that the context of the *Handschu* decree was the historic misdirection of the NYPD in surveillance of individuals and political groups, including such venerable organizations as the NAACP and the ACLU. Moreover, the files created about the members of these organizations and others under investigation for their political activities were then used in extralegal ways, by disseminating information to discredit individuals with employers, licensing agencies, and bar admission committees. In a pattern too familiar in other parts of the country, the NYPD expanded

---

[21] 605 F. Supp. 1384 (S.D.N.Y. 1985), *aff'd* 787 F.2d 828 (2d Cir. 1986).

beyond collection of information and used infiltrators as *agents provocateurs* to disrupt the activities of political organizations and to facilitate the arrests of organizational activists.

Shortly after *Handschu* was filed as a class action in 1971, the Senate Select Committee to Study Governmental Operations with Respect to Intelligence Activities issued its final report identifying "abuses committed by federal agencies . . . comparable to those described in the *Handschu* complaint . . . [which] demonstrated that the history of such abuse was too systemic and widespread to be regarded merely as episodic and as the unintentional consequence of occasional over zealousness."[22]

Handschu resulted in a settlement and a consent decree in 1985. The decree prohibited the NYPD from investigating political activities unless specific information had been received by the police department that a person or group engaged in political activity is engaged in, about to engage in, or has threatened to engage in conduct that constitutes a crime. The decree also imposed procedural limitations as a check against abuse and as a vehicle for maintaining a paper trail in the event that violations of the guidelines were to arise.

In September 2002, New York City asked to modify the decree and to eliminate both the substantive limitations and the procedural safeguards of the *Handschu* decree, although the city made no showing that the decree had hindered or would interfere with appropriate investigations. Nevertheless, Senior U.S. District Judge Charles S. Haight agreed to lower the threshold for investigation of political organizations and removed the specific procedural requirements of the earlier decree so that investigations could be ordered at lower ranks in the department and without any outside reviewing authority or paper trail.[23]

Within a few days of its adoption, the NYPD disobeyed the terms of the modified decree. On February 15, 2003, the NYPD prevented many from getting to the site of a large antiwar demonstration, leading to some 350 arrests, mostly for disorderly conduct. While lawyers waited outside police headquarters unable to enter the building to meet with their clients, the police interrogated the arrestees about their political activities based on a Demonstration Debriefing Form, which asked about the organizational affiliation of those arrested, the schools that they attended, and any prior demonstration history.

These interrogations suggest a return to the familiar pattern of information gathering in which those who engage in political protest and dissent are to be made the subject of political dossiers, and in which accountability for their actions is minimal.[24]

---

[22] Senate Select Comm. to Study Governmental Operations with Respect to Intelligence Activities, Final Report, S. REP. No. 755, 94th Cong., 2d Sess. (1976).

[23] In February 2003, U.S. District Court Judge Charles S. Haight, Jr., approved substantial modifications to the consent decree that had limited the NYPD's ability to investigate political activity. He also ordered that the NYPD adopt internal guidelines to ensure that the NYPD did not violate people's rights under the modifications. Handschu v. Special Services Div., 2003 U.S. Dist. LEXIS 3643 (S.D.N.Y.). On March 12, 2003, the judge approved the new guidelines that require the NYPD to maintain records of investigation, but no longer require it to submit evidence justifying investigation of political groups to an independent authority prior to commencing the investigation. Handschu v. Special Services Div., 2003 U.S. Dist. LEXIS 13811 (S.D.N.Y.).

[24] In a letter dated February 3, 2004, Stephen L. Hammerman, deputy commissioner of legal matters, New York City Police Department, wrote in response to this written testimony: "The comments of Arthur N. Eisenberg inaccurately mischaracterize not only the history of the Handschu case but also the recent litigation surrounding it. Because the old Handschu guidelines seriously hampered the investigation of activities engaged in during the preparation stage for terrorist activity when such preparations were made under the cover of First Amendment activity, (as they were in the case of the World Trade Center bombing in 1993), the NYPD applied to the court for a modification. After a highly contested litiga-

Robert J. Freeman, *Executive Director, New York Department of State Committee on Open Government*

Mr. Freeman explained that the basic principle underlying the New York Freedom of Information and Open Meetings Law is that access to government information is required unless disclosure would do identifiable harm.[25] In contrast, it was suggested that many of the measures taken since September 11 reflect an overreaction. For example, under the Homeland Security Act, "critical infrastructure information" is protected from disclosure.[26] Much "critical infrastructure information," however, is included in records that have long been public, such as maps.

Moreover, under heightened security policies, if government obtains information from private businesses that relates to critical infrastructure or trade secrets, that information must be kept confidential forever—there is no consideration of the harm that could arise from releasing the information. Under New York law, information submitted by a commercial enterprise that would harm its competitive position may be withheld. The impact of disclosure often changes over time. New York law imposes no need for permanent secrecy. Revelation of trade secrets that could lead to commercial injury at one point in time may years later be outdated. In that instance, the harmful effects of disclosure would have disappeared.

Much of what has been done by regulation and by statute since September 11, 2001, has been the result of knee jerk reactions. There has been little in-depth consideration of the impact of the changes. Mr. Freeman stated the position of his office that there is no need for an extensive revision of the state records access statute in order to protect against terrorism. Dealing effectively with terrorism is unquestionably critical, and the existing exceptions provide government with the ability to protect against inappropriate or injurious disclosures in the aftermath of 9/11.

He noted that although state law might appear insufficient to protect public safety, judicial interpretations have provided the necessary and appropriate safeguards. For example, in Section 87(2)(f) of the Freedom of Information Law,[27] an exception from disclosure applies when disclosure *would* endanger life or safety. He indicated that the courts have interpreted this standard in a manner that ensures public safety, effectively substituting a standard that records may be withheld when disclosure *could* endanger public safety. He described similar commonsense applications by the state's highest court

---

tion presided over by the Honorable Charles S. Haight, the court agreed that modification was inappropriate. Mr. Eisenberg's allegation that the NYPD violated the new Handschu guidelines within days of their becoming effective must be rejected since that same argument was made vigorously to Judge Haight who made no such finding. Mr. Eisenberg's obvious bias is evident in his assumption without a scrap of factual support, that the NYPD is gathering information about political dissent where there is no law enforcement purpose. The NYPD continues to deal with the terrorism issue while rigorously adhering to the new Handschu guidelines."

[25] NY CLS Pub. 0 § 87(f) (2003).

[26] Section 214(a)(1) of the Homeland Security Act of 2002, Pub. L. 107-296, 116 Stat. 2135 (2002), provides that "critical infrastructure that is voluntarily submitted to a covered Federal agency for use by that agency regarding the security of critical infrastructure and protected systems . . . shall be exempt from disclosure under the Freedom of Information Act. This provision, subtitled as the Critical Infrastructure Act of 2002, grants authority to impose a fine, up to a year of imprisonment, or both, as well as removal from employment, upon any government offender who discloses this protected infrastructure information. The Department of Homeland Security has issued proposed rules for 6 C.F.R. part 29 to implement this provision. Procedures for Handling Critical Infrastructure Information, 68 Fed. Reg. 18524 (2003). These procedures do not apply to, or affect any requirement pertaining to, information that must be submitted to a Federal agency or pertaining to the obligation of any Federal agency to disclose such information under FOIA."

[27] "Each agency shall, in accordance with its published rules, make available for public inspection and copying all records, except that such agency may deny access to records or portion thereof that . . . (f) if disclosed could endanger the life or safety of any person." NY CLS Pub. 0 § 87(f) (2003).

with respect to access to law enforcement records, including internal protocols that would reveal investigative techniques.

Mr. Freeman also noted that the state records access law has been amended to keep up with the times. For example, the statute was recently amended to ensure that state and local governments have a means to deny access to records that would threaten the security of electronic information systems. His conclusion regarding the adequacy of current state laws in the post-9/11 environment is that the existing exceptions to rights of access clearly provide government agencies the authority to withhold "critical infrastructure information" and similar materials involving private entities when disclosure would be damaging to the competitive position of those entities or inimical to the public interest in safety and security.[28]

Michael Wishnie, *Professor, New York University School of Law*

Professor Wishnie stated that the relation between federal, state, and local law enforcement agencies has been radically and, in his view, illegally changed with respect to enforcement of immigration violations.

Before September 11, 2001, the U.S. Department of Justice interpreted federal law to *prohibit* state and local police from involvement in civil immigration arrests.[29] The department interpreted the relevant statutes to permit state and local criminal immigration arrests if, and only if, authorized to do so by state and local law.

In 1996, Congress created a procedure so that states could agree to participate in criminal immigration arrests as a prerequisite to participating in immigration enforcement.[30] Those procedures required training and supervision by the federal Immigration and Naturalization Service (now the Bureau of Customs and Border Protection), and as recently as one year before the tragedies of 9/11, New York State Attorney General Eliot Spitzer said that under state law, state and local police could not make civil immigration arrests. After 9/11, however, the Justice Department rescinded the opinion letters it had issued since the 1970s and decided there was inherent authority for state and local police to make immigration violation arrests.

Additionally, a 1930 federal statute limits the information that can go into the National Criminal Information Center (NCIC) database. Until Attorney General Ashcroft recently modified NCIC database procedures, immigration data was not entered into the national NCIC database. Accordingly, when police stopped an individual and called for information from the database, immigration infor-

---

[28] "Each agency shall, in accordance with its published rules, make available for public inspection and copying all records, except that such agency may deny access to records or portion thereof that: . . . (i) if disclosed, would jeopardize an agency's capacity to guarantee the security of its information technology assets, such assets encompassing both electronic information systems and infrastructures." NY CLS Pub. 0 § 87(i) (2003).

[29] Memorandum for the United States Attorney, Southern District of California, from Teresa Wynn Roseborough, Deputy Assistant Attorney General, Office of Legal Counsel, Re: Assistance by State and Local Police in Apprehending Illegal Aliens (Feb. 5, 1996). This opinion was overruled by an unpublished opinion. Possible justification for this opinion is United States v. Salinas-Calderon, 728 F.2d 1298 (10th Cir. 1984), which found that local law enforcement officers have general investigatory powers to inquire into "immigration violations." In United States v. Vazquez-Alvarez, 176 F.3d 1294 (10th Cir. 1999), the court upheld a police officer's arrest for unlawful presence in the country, a civil immigration offense.

[30] Section 133 of the Illegal Immigration Reform and Immigrant Responsibility Act of 1996, Pub. L. No. 104-208, 110 Stat. 3009–646 (amended 8 U.S.C. § 1103(a)), allows the Attorney General to enter into agreements to delegate immigration powers to local police during a period of declared "mass influx of aliens," but only through negotiated agreements, documented through Memoranda of Understanding.

mation would not have been included. Now, however, the Justice Department downloads civil immigration information into the NCIC database.[31] At the time any local officer accesses the database for information about a specific person, he or she will get this information, and New York City Police Commissioner Kelly has stated that the NYPD will make arrests for immigration violations in New York City. The result has been illegal arrests; that is, arrests which are unlawful under the federal NCIC statute.[32]

---

[31] 8 U.S.C. §§ 1105, 1379 (2004).

[32] In a letter dated February 3, 2004, Stephen L. Hammerman, deputy commissioner of legal matters, New York City Police Department, wrote in response to this written testimony: "The comments of Michael Wishnie include a statement that Police Commissioner Kelly has stated that the NYPD will make arrests for immigration violations in New York City. Commissioner Kelly's statement is recited out of context. The NYPD does cooperate with the Bureau of Immigration and Customs Enforcement, to the extent that an NCIC check of a person who has been detained for other reasons reveals that he or she is wanted by federal authorities for an immigration violation that also constitutes a federal crime. It is entirely appropriate that such criminal status should be communicated to federal authorities. It is our understanding that only those whose immigration offenses that carry criminal penalties are entered into the NCIC database. Therefore, our notification to federal authorities when a person comes into NYPD custody and is listed as an immigration violator in NCIC does not mean that the NYPD is making arrests for immigration violations, and the arrests that are made are not illegal."

Chapter 3: Concerns and Observations

The New York Advisory Committee expresses the following concerns and conclusions based on presentations from the community forum:

Racial and Ethnic Profiling

There are parallels between the racial profiling of Japanese Americans during World War II, African Americans and Hispanic Americans before 9/11, and Muslims, Arabs, and South Asians after 9/11. Racial profiling has been statistically proven by government studies, such as the New York State Attorney General's 1999 study of stop-and-frisk practices, to be an ineffective law enforcement tool for identifying criminal conduct. Beyond law enforcement acts of racial profiling related to drug prevention and street crime, racial profiling has taken on new dimensions targeting Muslims, Arabs, and South Asians regarding business license violations, financial transactions abroad, or international travel at airports. Furthermore, members of the general public in New York have also engaged in racial targeting in the form of hate violence directed toward Muslims, Arabs, and South Asians. In some instances of hate violence, there has been no response by law enforcement authorities. Such broad-based practices of racial profiling have had the effect of instilling fear among members of targeted religious, ethnic, and racial groups, particularly of the law enforcement authorities sworn to protect them.

Observations:

1. Legislation should be passed that would establish a viable auditing system to ensure the availability of accurate race and ethnicity data for monitoring racial and ethnic profiling.

2. Investigations into the failures of the police to intervene to protect Muslims, Arabs, and South Asians from harassment; the violation of confidentiality of Taxi and Limousine Commission records pertaining to immigrant taxi drivers; and other matters related to incidents of racial and ethnic profiling and harassment need to be conducted promptly and thoroughly, and the results made public.

3. The Transportation Security Administration should revise "no fly" list procedures to permit passengers to challenge their inclusion on the list, and in the cases of persons with the same name as a person who would legitimately be detained, to establish a mechanism for the innocent flyer to establish that the "no fly" order does not pertain to him or her.

4. The Office of Foreign Asset Control of the U.S. Department of Treasury should establish procedures to provide for the immediate review of financial transactions interrupted under its requirements, resulting in depriving innocent persons of their assets.

5. All security and law enforcement agencies should develop ongoing programs for out-reach to minority communities who have been affected, particularly in the post-9/11 envi-ronment—not only to assure those communities that they are protected under the law, but to ensure an openness of communication with those communities, which is essential to national security.

Border Crossing Issues

After the federal Call-In Special Registration program was initiated, many Muslim, Arab, and South Asian individuals and families attempted to cross the border from Buffalo or Plattsburgh, New York, into Canada to apply for asylum with Citizenship and Immigration Canada. Citizenship and Immigra-tion Canada could not quickly accommodate the increased numbers of asylum seekers and sent many back to the United States to wait for their scheduled appointment date. U.S. Customs and Border Protection authorities placed many "kicked back" asylum seekers in detention for deportation pro-ceedings with excessive bonds as a condition of release. In addition, outbound checks by U.S. au-thorities resulted in the detention and placement into deportation proceedings of other Canadian-bound asylum seekers. These actions deprived the asylum seekers of access to Citizenship and Immi-gration Canada and the protection this access potentially provides.

Observation:

6. If a Canadian-bound asylum seeker is directed back to the United States by the Canadian government, provisions such as administrative voluntary departure or parole should be utilized so that the individual remains in one immigration system, not two. If Canadian-bound asylum seekers are detained in the United States while en route to the border, they should be paroled and allowed to proceed to the border to begin their claim and, once the claim is initiated, they should be allowed to return to their place of residence in the United States, particularly when an individual can illustrate clear intent to go to Canada or has family or other connections there. The process of setting bonds on detained asylum seekers should be reviewed and a consistent policy be put in place.

The Call-In Special Registration Program

The federal Call-In Special Registration program requiring male nationals 16 years and older from predominantly Muslim countries to register was a program rooted in racial profiling, targeting Mus-lims, Arabs, and South Asians, and raising constitutional concerns. The program ceased after nation-als from predominantly Muslim countries had registered. In New York City, many people required to go through special registration were denied access to counsel during critical stages of the registration process, particularly while interrogated by the investigations unit of the Bureau of Immigration and Customs Enforcement of the U.S. Department of Homeland Security, when they were most vulner-able. Families of registrants, who were detained and subjected to closed immigration hearings by immigration judges, were not informed of the detained registrants' whereabouts.

Observations:

7. The Call-In Special Registration program should not be expanded. The program has questionably served national security interests and, in fact, may have been counterpro-ductive to such interests. Those who registered were persons seeking to comply in good

faith with the law, not terrorists in hiding. The program has alienated many members of Muslim, Arab, and South Asian communities who believe they have been targeted based solely on their national origin and religious beliefs. Because of fear engendered by racial profiling, many members of these communities avoid interaction with law enforcement authorities.

8. Immigration hearings held in connection with special registration should have independent judges, be open to the public, and afford appropriate access to and representation by legal counsel.

Legal Issues After 9/11: Due Process, Checks and Balances, and Access to Records

With the passage of the USA Patriot Act and the creation of the Department of Homeland Security, immigration authorities have had to exercise unprecedented enforcement responsibilities. Many foreign-born persons were denied hearings and detained without having been charged. Many of those detained have been unable to obtain release on bond, and have been held for prolonged periods after issuance of final deportation orders. These practices have been accompanied by a significant change in federal law enforcement agencies' relationships with state and local agencies and airport security officials—a change that risks establishing a new generation of racial profiling in which a person's ethnicity or national origin significantly increases his or her chance of being scrutinized by local law enforcement or detained at an airport. And, in a break with longstanding practices from a decades-old federal statutory requirement, local law enforcement agencies are now poised to make arrests for violations, including minor violations, of immigration laws.

Most of the persons affected by these policy and structural changes have been Muslims, South Asians, and Middle Eastern foreign nationals. In each instance, there have been no practical means of judicial or legislative recourse, creating a widespread feeling in these communities, among citizens and noncitizens alike, that they have been unfairly singled out and are powerless. Consequently, there has been an increasing reluctance by members of these communities to assist in providing information vital to the country's security needs.

New York City has a history recognized by the courts of carrying out excessive surveillance practices against religious and political organizations. Those practices were restricted in 1985 under the *Handschu* consent decree, a court-approved agreement between the parties that had worked well for 17 years. On the basis of a need for increased security measures after 9/11, however, New York City sought court approval to modify the decree to eliminate both substantive limitations and procedural safeguards. Without requiring a showing that the decree had hindered or would interfere with investigations, the court agreed to lower the threshold for investigation of political organizations and modified specific procedural requirements in the consent decree. Investigations can now be ordered at lower ranks within the NYPD and without review by any outside authority or the establishing of a paper trail. Moreover, based on similar fears over heightened security needs, proposals have been made to restrict public access to records. Security measures are indeed a high priority. However, restricting public access to records by shifting the presumption that government records are subject to disclosure to one against such disclosure may unnecessarily reduce the accountability of the government through monitoring and surveillance. Moreover, according to the head of the state's Committee on Open Government, existing disclosure protections are adequate to protect public security and have worked quite well.

Observations:

9. The distinction between civil enforcement and criminal arrests must be maintained so that persons charged with crimes are not deprived of the due process protections they would be normally afforded in the criminal justice system, and conversely so that persons charged with immigration violations are afforded the full procedural safeguards established under the nation's system for addressing alleged immigration violations.

10. A fully independent oversight body should be created outside the Department of Homeland Security to report on, and to monitor, the implementation of security measures taken in conjunction with the Homeland Security Act, including policies with respect to racial profiling, "no fly" lists, financial assets control, due process in immigration proceedings (including, in particular, any future Call-In Special Registration programs), the sharing of intelligence information between federal and local law enforcement agencies, surveillance and monitoring of religious and political organizations, and access to public records.

11. In addition to the oversight role to be played by official bodies, a prudent level of public accountability through a rational level of access to public records is an essential element to preserving confidence in the government. Neither state nor federal records access laws should be made more restrictive based simply on the untested premise that doing so is essential to addressing the nation's increased security needs. Standards should be established that continue the presumption that records must be disclosed in the absence of a particularized determination that access to the record undermines a legitimate security interest, and when portions of the requested documents do not jeopardize such a security interest, those portions should continue to be made public.

Appendix

Department of Justice

TUESDAY, JUNE 17, 2003
WWW.USDOJ.GOV

(202) 514-2008
TDD (202) 514-1888

FACT SHEET
RACIAL PROFILING

"It's wrong, and we will end it in America. In so doing, we will not hinder the work of our nation's brave police officers. They protect us every day -- often at great risk. But by stopping the abuses of a few, we will add to the public confidence our police officers earn and deserve." --President George W. Bush, Feb. 27, 2001

"This administration... has been opposed to racial profiling and has done more to indicate its opposition than ever in history. The President said it's wrong and we'll end it in America, and I subscribe to that. Using race... as a proxy for potential criminal behavior is unconstitutional, and it undermines law enforcement by undermining the confidence that people can have in law enforcement." --Attorney General John Ashcroft, Feb. 28, 2002

Defining the Problem:
Racial Profiling Is Wrong and Will Not Be Tolerated

Racial profiling sends the dehumanizing message to our citizens that they are judged by the color of their skin and harms the criminal justice system by eviscerating the trust that is necessary if law enforcement is to effectively protect our communities.

- **America Has a Moral Obligation to Prohibit Racial Profiling.** Race-based assumptions in law enforcement perpetuate negative racial stereotypes that are harmful to our diverse democracy, and materially impair our efforts to maintain a fair and just society. As Attorney General John Ashcroft said, racial profiling creates a "lose-lose" situation because it destroys the potential for underlying trust that "should support the administration of justice as a societal objective, not just as a law enforcement objective."

- **The Overwhelming Majority of Federal Law Enforcement Officers Perform Their Jobs with Dedication, Fairness and Honor, But Any Instance of Racial Profiling by a Few Damages Our Criminal Justice System.** The vast majority of federal law enforcement officers are hard-working public servants who perform a dangerous job with dedication, fairness and honor. However, when law enforcement practices are perceived to be biased or unfair, the general public, and especially minority communities, are less willing to trust and confide in officers, report crimes, be witnesses at trials, or serve on juries.

- **Racial Profiling Is Discrimination, and It Taints the Entire Criminal Justice System.** Racial profiling rests on the erroneous assumption that any particular individual of one race or ethnicity is more likely to engage in misconduct than any particular individual of other races or ethnicities.

Taking Steps to Ban Racial Profiling:
**Due to the Seriousness of Racial Profiling, the Justice Department
Has Developed Guidelines to Make Clear that It Is
Prohibited in Federal Law Enforcement**

- **President Bush Has Directed that Racial Profiling Be Formally Banned.** In his February 27, 2001, Address to a Joint Session of Congress, President George W. Bush declared that racial profiling is "wrong and we will end it in America." He directed the Attorney General to review the use by federal law enforcement authorities of race as a factor in conducting stops, searches and other law enforcement investigative procedures. The Attorney General, in turn, instructed the Civil Rights Division to develop guidance for federal officials to ensure an end to racial profiling in federal law enforcement.

- **The Bush Administration Is the First to Take Action to Ban Racial Profiling in Federal Law Enforcement.** The guidance has been sent to all federal law enforcement agencies and is effective immediately. Federal agencies will review their policies and procedures to ensure compliance.

- **The Guidance Requires More Restrictions on the Use of Race by Federal Law Enforcement than Does the Constitution.** The guidance in many cases imposes *more* restrictions on the use of race and ethnicity in federal law enforcement than the Constitution requires. This guidance prohibits racial profiling in federal law enforcement practices without hindering the important work of our nation's public safety officials, particularly the intensified anti-terrorism efforts precipitated by the attacks of September 11, 2001.

- **Prohibiting Racial Profiling in Routine or Spontaneous Activities in Domestic Law Enforcement:** In making routine or spontaneous law enforcement decisions, such as ordinary traffic stops, federal law enforcement officers may *not* use race or ethnicity to any degree, except that officers may rely on race and ethnicity if a specific suspect description exists. This prohibition applies even where the use of race or ethnicity might otherwise be lawful.

    ✓ **Routine Patrol Duties Must Be Carried Out Without Consideration of Race.** Federal law enforcement agencies and officers sometimes engage in law enforcement activities, such as traffic and foot patrols, that generally do not involve either the ongoing investigation of specific criminal activities or the prevention of catastrophic events or harm to the national security. Rather, their activities are typified by spontaneous action in response to the activities of individuals whom they happen to encounter in the course of their patrols and about whom they have no information other than their observations. These general enforcement responsibilities should be carried out without *any* consideration of race or ethnicity.

        - *Example*: While parked by the side of the highway, a federal officer notices that nearly all vehicles on the road are exceeding the posted speed limit. Although each such vehicle is committing an infraction that would legally justify a stop, the officer may not use race or ethnicity as a factor in deciding which motorists to pull over. Likewise, the officer may not use race or ethnicity in deciding which detained motorists to ask to consent to a search of their vehicles.

✓ **Stereotyping Certain Races as Having a Greater Propensity to Commit Crimes Is Absolutely Prohibited.** Some have argued that overall discrepancies in crime rates among racial groups could justify using race as a factor in general traffic enforcement activities and would produce a greater number of arrests for non-traffic offenses (*e.g.*, narcotics trafficking). We emphatically reject this view. It is patently unacceptable and thus prohibited under this guidance for federal law enforcement officers to engage in racial profiling.

✓ **Acting on Specific Suspect Identification Does Not Constitute Impermissible Stereotyping.** The situation is different when a federal officer acts on the personal identifying characteristics of potential suspects, including age, sex, ethnicity or race. Common sense dictates that when a victim or witness describes the assailant as being of a particular race, authorities may properly limit their search for suspects to persons of that race. In such circumstances, the federal officer is not acting based on a generalized assumption about persons of different races; rather, the officer is helping locate a specific individual previously identified as involved in crime.

- *Example:* While parked by the side of the highway, a federal officer receives an "All Points Bulletin" to be on the look-out for a fleeing bank robbery suspect, a man of a particular race and particular hair color in his 30s driving a blue automobile. The officer may use this description, including the race of the particular suspect, in deciding which speeding motorists to pull over.

- **Prohibiting Racial Profiling in Federal Law Enforcement Activities Related to Specific Investigations**: In conducting activities in connection with a specific investigation, federal law enforcement officers may consider race and ethnicity only to the extent that there is trustworthy information, relevant to the locality or time frame, that links persons of a particular race or ethnicity to an identified criminal incident, scheme, or organization. This standard applies even where the use of race or ethnicity might otherwise be lawful.

✓ **Acting on Specific Information Does Not Constitute Impermissible Stereotyping.** Often federal officers have specific information, based on trustworthy sources, to "be on the lookout" for specific individuals identified at least in part by race or ethnicity. In such circumstances, the officer is not acting based on a generalized assumption about persons of different races; rather, the officer is helping locate specific individuals previously identified as involved in crime.

- *Example:* In connection with a new initiative to increase drug arrests, federal authorities begin aggressively enforcing speeding, traffic, and other public area laws in a neighborhood predominantly occupied by people of a single race. The choice of neighborhood was not based on the number of 911 calls, number of arrests, or other pertinent reporting data specific to that area, but only on the general assumption that more drug-related crime occurs in that neighborhood because of its racial composition. This effort would be *improper* because it is based on generalized stereotypes.

- *Example*: The victim of an assault at a local university describes her assailant as a young male of a particular race with a cut on his right hand. The investigation focuses on whether any students at the university fit the victim's description. Here investigators are properly relying on a description given by the victim, part of which included the assailant's race. Although the ensuing investigation affects students of a particular race, that investigation is not undertaken with a discriminatory purpose. Thus use of race as a factor in the investigation, in this instance, is permissible.

✓ **Reliance Upon Generalized Stereotypes Continues to Be Absolutely Forbidden.** Use of race or ethnicity is permitted only when the federal officer is pursuing a specific lead concerning the identifying characteristics of persons involved in an *identified* criminal activity. The rationale underlying this concept carefully limits its reach. In order to qualify as a legitimate investigative lead, the following must be true:

- The information must be relevant to the locality or time frame of the criminal activity;

- The information must be trustworthy; and,

- The information concerning identifying characteristics must be tied to a particular criminal incident, a particular criminal scheme, or a particular criminal organization.

- *Example*: The FBI is investigating the murder of a known gang member and has information that the shooter is a member of a rival gang. The FBI knows that the members of the rival gang are exclusively members of a certain ethnicity. This information, however, is not suspect-specific because there is no description of the particular assailant. But because authorities have reliable, locally relevant information linking a rival group with a distinctive ethnic character to the murder, federal law enforcement officers could properly consider ethnicity in conjunction with other appropriate factors in the course of conducting their investigation. Agents could properly decide to focus on persons dressed in a manner consistent with gang activity, but ignore persons dressed in that manner who do not appear to be members of that particular ethnicity.

- *Example*: While investigating a car theft ring that dismantles cars and ships the parts for sale in other states, the FBI is informed by local authorities that it is common knowledge locally that most car thefts in that area are committed by individuals of a particular race. In this example, although the source (local police) is trustworthy, and the information potentially verifiable with reference to arrest statistics, there is no particular incident- or scheme- specific information linking individuals of that race to the particular interstate ring the FBI is investigating. Thus, agents could not use ethnicity as a factor in making law enforcement decisions in this investigation.

Taking Steps to Balance National Security Concerns:
The Justice Department's Policy Guidance Ensures that Federal Law Enforcement Continues to Have the Tools Needed to Identify Terrorist Threats and Stop Potential Catastrophic Attacks

- **Federal Law Enforcement Will Continue Terrorist Identification.** Since the terrorist attacks on September 11, 2001, the President has emphasized that federal law enforcement personnel must use every legitimate tool to prevent future attacks, protect our nation's borders, and deter those who would cause devastating harm to our country and its people through the use of biological or chemical weapons, other weapons of mass destruction, suicide hijackings, or any other means.

  - ✓ Therefore, the racial profiling guidance recognizes that race and ethnicity may be used in terrorist identification, but only to the extent permitted by the nation's laws and the Constitution. The policy guidance emphasizes that, even in the national security context, the constitutional restriction on use of generalized stereotypes remains.

- **Federal Law Enforcement Must Adhere to Limitations Imposed by the Constitution.** In investigating or preventing threats to national security or other catastrophic events (including the performance of duties related to air transportation security), or in enforcing laws protecting the integrity of the nation's borders, federal law enforcement officers may not consider race or ethnicity except to the extent permitted by the Constitution and laws of the United States.

  - ✓ **The Constitution Prohibits Consideration of Race or Ethnicity in Law Enforcement Decisions in All But the Most Exceptional Instances.** Given the incalculably high stakes involved in such investigations, federal law enforcement officers who are protecting national security or preventing catastrophic events (as well as airport security screeners) may consider race, ethnicity, alienage, and other relevant factors. Constitutional provisions limiting government action on the basis of race are wide-ranging and provide substantial protections at every step of the investigative and judicial process. Accordingly, this policy will honor the rule of law and promote vigorous protection of our national security.

  - ✓ **Federal Law Enforcement Must Guard Against Uncertain Threats of Terrorism.** Because terrorist organizations might aim to engage in unexpected acts of catastrophic violence in any available part of the country (indeed, in multiple places simultaneously, if possible), there can be no expectation that the information must be specific to a particular locale or even to a particular identified scheme.

- **Even in the National Security Context, Reliance Upon Generalized Stereotypes Is Restricted by the Constitution.** For example, at the security entrance to a federal courthouse, a man who appears to be of a particular ethnicity properly submits his briefcase for x-ray screening and passes through the metal detector. The inspection of the briefcase reveals nothing amiss. The man does not activate the metal detector, and there is nothing suspicious about his activities or appearance. Absent any threat warning or other particular reason to suspect that those of the man's apparent ethnicity pose a heightened danger to the courthouse, the federal security screener may not order the man to undergo a further inspection solely because of his apparent ethnicity.

  ✓ *Example*: U.S. intelligence sources report that Middle Eastern terrorists are planning to use commercial jetliners as weapons by hijacking them at an airport in California during the next week. Before allowing men appearing to be of Middle Eastern origin to board commercial airplanes in California airports during the next week, Transportation Security Administration personnel, and other federal and state authorities, may subject them to heightened scrutiny.

  ✓ *Example*: The FBI receives reliable information that persons affiliated with a foreign ethnic insurgent group intend to use suicide bombers to assassinate that country's president and his entire entourage during an official visit to the United States. Federal law enforcement may appropriately focus investigative attention on identifying members of that ethnic insurgent group who may be present and active in the United States and who, based on other available information, might conceivably be involved in planning some such attack during the state visit.

www.ingramcontent.com/pod-product-compliance
Lightning Source LLC
Chambersburg PA
CBHW081232170526
45165CB00009B/3043